Contents

8/12

DATE DUE FOR RETURN

Renewals

Hodder Education

338 Euston Road, London NW1 3BH

Hodder Education is an Hachette UK company

First published in UK 2011 by Hodder Education

This edition published 2011

Copyright © 2011 Julie Gray

Database right Hodder Education (makers)

The moral rights of the author have been asserted

British Library Cataloguing in Publication Data: a catalogue record for this title is available from the British Library.

10 9 8 7 6 5 4 3 2

The publisher has used its best endeavours to ensure that any website addresses referred to in this book are correct and active at the time of going to press. However, the publisher and the author have no responsibility for the websites and can make no guarantee that a site will remain live or that the content will remain relevant, decent or appropriate.

The publisher has made every effort to mark as such all words which it believes to be trademarks. The publisher should also like to make it clear that the presence of a word in the book, whether marked or unmarked, in no way affects its legal status as a trademark.

Every reasonable effort has been made by the publisher to trace the copyright holders of material in this book. Any errors or omissions should be notified in writing to the publisher, who will endeavour to rectify the situation for any reprints and future editions.

Hachette UK's policy is to use papers that are natural, renewable and recyclable products and made from wood grown in sustainable forests. The logging and manufacturing processes are expected to conform to the environmental regulations of the country of origin.

www.hoddereducation.co.uk

Typeset by Cenveo Publisher Services

Printed in Great Britain by CPI Group (UK) Ltd, Croydon, CR0 4YY

Also available in ebook

Meet the author

Welcome to *Interview Success – Get the Edge*!

Understanding what a particular employer is looking for, and clearly putting across how well you meet their needs, will give you the edge in any interview. It's simply an extension of the process you started with your CV: putting yourself in an employer's shoes.

If your CV made it out of the pile and onto the interview short-list, you're on the right track. The interview is to reassure your prospective employer that you told the truth about your skills and experience, will be more of an asset to them than other candidates, and are worth investing in. It also helps if the interviewer can see that you are not impossible to get along with, unwilling to attend to personal hygiene, or psychotic.

The interviewer will assess how you look (and smell), behave and communicate. It will help if you are aware of what you and your body may be telling them before, during and after the interview.

My take on interviewing comes from both sides: I worked in sales, recruitment and marketing before becoming a professional CV writer. My rounded perspective on the interview process is tempered with a healthy dash of cynicism, based on a practical appreciation of what works in the real world.

Whatever the latest trend, whether you are a first-time interviewee or experienced career ladder climber, there are plenty of useful tips and tricks in these pages to help you get the edge over other candidates. The most important trick of all is to prepare, and do it well.

Best of luck!

Julie Gray

In one minute

Interviews are terribly unfair; coming second wins you nothing. Getting the edge over everyone else requires solid preparation:

1 **researching** the company and the job, and how you will fit
2 **thinking** about your answers in depth – *before* the interview
3 **knowing** what to expect, how to dress and how to behave.

Preparation takes time; time that you may feel you can't spare. But being well prepared is proof that you are genuinely keen on the job. Good preparation will also help you to feel more confident, be more positive and perform better.

To decide if this book can help you, ask yourself three questions:

Q1: *Have you thought about, and do you genuinely want, the job you're applying for?*

Why waste precious time on a job that you don't really, really want?

Q2: *Do you really want to teach yourself better interview skills?*

You won't find a set of generic answers here that you can learn by heart.

Convincing an employer that you're the best person for the job means showing you know:

1 exactly what the company is looking for
2 which specific benefits you can bring to them
3 how well you'll fit into the team and the company.

Q3: *Will you make the effort to prepare your own interview approach, answers and questions?*

If you do, you will end up with a customized interview crib sheet: a mixture of unique statements and answers that together will help you explain to an interviewer all they need to know about you.

If you can answer yes to all three questions, then this book is for you.

How to use this book

By all means read this book from cover to cover if you have time, but if you have an interview in…

1 DAY
2–3 DAYS
1 WEEK (or more)
…and you're not sure what you should be preparing, or how to prioritize it, the following guide may help to get you started on the most important areas.

Background

1 DAY – 10 minutes
2–3 DAYS – 20 minutes
1 WEEK – 30 minutes
Depending on your level of experience, you may wish to skip this step entirely. For first-time interviewees, or those attending a certain type of interview (e.g. a group interview) for the first time, it may help you to know a little bit more about what to expect and what the employer is likely to be looking for. There's a useful summary of interview types and formats in **Chapter 3.**

Preparation

1 DAY – 2.5 hours
2–3 DAYS – 5 hours
1 WEEK – 10 hours (do you really want this job?)
The following four tasks should be possible to complete in 2.5 to 3 hours for those most rushed, or you can scale them up according to how much time you have available.

PRIORITY 1: RESEARCH THE COMPANY

1 DAY – 30 mins +
2–3 DAYS – 1 hour +
1 WEEK – 2 hours +

Yes, this comes before swotting up on possible questions. The single greatest way to impress an interviewer is to convince them that you really want this job and to work for this company above all else. Research can also guide you in prioritizing which selling points this employer is going to be most interested in. **Chapter 6** gives more detail on how to research an organization.

PRIORITY 2: WRITE A STATEMENT TO ANSWER: 'TELL ME ABOUT YOURSELF.'

1 DAY – 20 mins +
2–3 DAYS – 45 mins +
1 WEEK – 1.5 hours +

This is one of the most common questions you will be asked at any interview; often one of the first, if not the first. Perhaps because it is such an innocent-seeming question, something that you could answer in almost any way you choose, it is also one that many people fall down on. Don't waste a perfect opportunity to make a brilliant first impression.

Please see **Chapter 10** for an example of a 'Tell me about yourself' statement, and related questions that this statement will help you to answer.

PRIORITY 3: WRITE A STATEMENT TO EXPLAIN: 'WHAT ATTRACTS YOU TO THIS JOB?'

1 DAY – 20 mins +
2–3 DAYS – 45 mins +
1 WEEK – 1.5 hours +

Not surprisingly, this is another very common question. It's your chance to show them you have given your application careful consideration. **Chapter 10** gives an example of a 'Tell me what attracts you to this job' statement, and related questions you can also answer using this statement.

PRIORITY 4: PREPARE ANSWERS TO THE MOST LIKELY QUESTIONS

1 DAY – 1.5 hours +
2–3 DAYS – 3 hours +
1 WEEK – 6 hours +

Opinion differs widely about what will come up in any interview but there are a number of 'core' questions – around 15 or so – that most interviewers are likely to ask. **Chapter 10** covers the 15 most common questions in more detail and how you should go about answering them in their various guises.

If you have some interview experience, and have already prepared suitable answers to these most likely questions, then try scanning the lists of further questions in **Chapters 11 to 16** and selecting the 15 that you'd least like to be asked. Yes, least like: the questions you dread most (or haven't thought about) are the ones that you'll probably be asked.

Action

1 DAY – 20 minutes +
2–3 DAYS – 45 minutes +
1 WEEK – 1.5 hours +

There are several practical things recommended to do before your interview: sort out a suitable outfit, plan your behaviour and become more aware of your communication. For more detailed advice about outfit choice and what your clothes may be saying about you, see **Chapter 19.**

Some basic techniques can improve your body language, and help you to feel calmer if you're nervous on the day – take a look at the confidence tricks you can try in **Chapter 20.**

Even with unlimited time, no one can prepare for every scenario. All you can do is think ahead to help you manage the unexpected without falling apart.

See **Chapter 24** for tips on how to:

▶ manage pre-interview crises, such as running late
▶ deal with difficult or scary interviewers
▶ recover from difficulties before the interview ends
▶ ensure you learn from every experience.

Part one

Background

1

Five things interviewers want to know about you

In this chapter you will learn about:
- *the five principal goals of the interviewer*
- *how, in outline, you should begin to respond to these goals.*

Whether the process is handled in one interview or across several, whether you are interviewed by the company itself or by a recruitment agency on its behalf, the information sought is always largely the same:

1 proof of CV claims
2 desire
3 personality
4 fit
5 cost.

Interviewers don't just want to hear you repeat what you put on your CV; they want you to demonstrate to them that what you said was true, that you really can do the job and do it well. They'll also be interested in whether you are genuinely committed to the job and the company.

The interview is a great opportunity for them to see for themselves what kind of a person you'll be like to work with. Based on that, they'll judge how well you're likely to get on with colleagues, management and the company environment in general.

Their final concern, if you appeal to them on all these other counts, will be how much it may cost to get you and to keep you.

1 Proof of the skills and experience on your CV

Hopefully, you didn't put anything on your CV that you can't prove. In this context, proof doesn't normally mean performing the skill on the spot, but giving strong examples of times you have done so.

For anything you included on your CV, ideally you will have already prepared two or more concrete examples of when you used that skill, drew from your experience, applied your knowledge, exhibited a behaviour/characteristic, or combined all of these to demonstrate competency. You may hear the expression 'competency interview' quite a lot as it is a popular interview format, but don't be put off by the terminology. All a competency interview really does is ask you for examples of how you've demonstrated your particular abilities; which is no more than you should be preparing anyway.

If something is not on your CV but *is* listed in the job advert criteria, then come up with two concrete examples of this skill or ability that you can give at interview. (Consider adding these to your generic CV, if appropriate, so you can easily call on them in future.)

If you cannot demonstrate that you meet a particular job criterion, don't waffle or bluff – just omit it. If questioned, be honest but move quickly on to the other relevant skills or experience you can bring to the job. If the criterion is considered critical by the interviewer, you could add your willingness to develop that skill, and give examples of other things you've quickly learned on the job.

It never hurts to show some self-awareness during this part of the interview: think about the process by which you developed each of your skills. Be prepared to talk about how you have learned through failure, as well as success, to work differently over time. Don't dwell on the failure part for very long, but it helps if you can acknowledge it. Interviewers tend to like people who can learn, develop and grow in value over time.

2 Desire

You would think it safe to assume that someone going to the effort of applying for a job and attending an interview would really want the job – but that's not always the case. Whether they're casting about for alternatives to see if it's worth jumping ship, or out of work and desperate to get back into it any way they can, there are always candidates who look fine on paper but just aren't really motivated by this particular opportunity.

Given the cost of recruiting new staff, interviewers are very curious to know how strong your desire is to work for them. They want to quickly weed out anyone who doesn't really, really want the job. These candidates will either turn a job offer down, leaving the interviewer chasing up second or third favourites, or may accept but move on again quite quickly.

The most common way for interviewers to assess the level of desire is to find out how much someone really knows about the job opportunity and the company as a whole – and whether they have properly thought out their next career move. You'll need to show them that you've really done your research and thought your position through carefully.

3 Personality

The interviewer can't tell whether you're going to be easy to work with or not. After all, although interview situations are often pressured, they are not exactly typical – and you'll also (hopefully) be on your best behaviour. A good interviewer will use several sources of information to predict what you're most likely going to be like to work with.

The first is how you come across during the interview. This perception starts to be built from the very first moment – how you look and how you greet the interviewer. Some interviewers also place considerable importance on how you handle any small talk about your journey, the weather, or the news, prior to the 'proper' questions beginning.

Another aspect that interviewers rely on to make their judgement of your personality is hearing how you have behaved in work situations in the past. When asked to explain how you've worked as part of a team, for example, they will be thinking about whether the behaviours you describe are likely to work well and be productive in this particular environment.

Equally, some interviewers like to ask how you *would* behave in a hypothetical situation that might arise. Your answer could indicate whether you would go about a particular task in a way that would suit their working style. However, whether this is a good predictor of future behaviour is debatable – candidates are likely to try and give the answer they think is most desirable, which may not reflect what they would actually do.

Finally, the 'perfect/worst' scenario is often used at interview to establish candidates' preferences and therefore working styles. You might be quizzed on which is the best or worst company you've ever worked for, and why. Or who would be your dream (or nightmare) boss and why.

Overstating your preferences can make you seem inflexible. If you describe your interviewer's working style by chance, and say you'd find that hell to work with, you are less likely to make round two than if you say you work well with any style of management but that certain behaviours inspire you more. If you feel very strongly about how you're managed, then it's probably better to identify a mismatch now, before you jump into the job.

4 Fit

This is closely linked to your personality and working style. The interviewer is trying to figure out, based on limited clues, whether you are likely to gel with the team around you and the organization's culture as a whole. They'll look at anything you give them from your appearance or background, your personality or working style, to your sense of humour or ambitions.

Yes, fit is a wholly subjective judgement. In many cases, it's unjust – some of these things have no real bearing on whether or not you could do the job well. You can't change who you are; and if you did, just to get this job, would you want to spend every working day pretending to be something you are not? What you can do is research the organization's culture, work out what type of person or qualities they seem to value most, and ensure you clearly put across those aspects of yourself.

5 Cost

Whether this is established at the first interview or a later interview (as is more common), if the interviewer feels you tick most of their boxes then the next relevant question is: What will they have to offer in order to get you, and keep you?

Interviewers will be able to glean some of the information they need from what you say. Knowing what responsibilities you currently have, and the salary you are or have been on, will give them a standard to compare against. Asking about your career ambitions may give them an indication of what motivates you.

You are more likely to be able to negotiate a higher salary, an improved package or support for training/qualifications, if you show you are not only qualified for the job but keen to get it and committed to the company in the longer term.

FOCAL POINTS

- Your interview is a chance to prove everything you've claimed: use examples.

- Show the interviewer you really want this particular job.

- Your personality may be judged in many ways; not all will be fair.

- Spell out to the interviewer why you'll be a good fit with his or her team.

- Sell yourself before you set a price for yourself.

- Sell yourself well, and the asking price could go higher.

2

How employers assess candidates

In this chapter you will learn about:
- *how interviewers judge the interviews*
- *how you can control the messages you send to the interviewer.*

Lawyer, judge and jury

Your interviewer will act a bit like lawyer, judge and jury all rolled into one:

▶ **Lawyer:** Interviewers cannot be sure of many things that you tell them – but, as they are in the business of assessing people, you can guarantee a good interviewer will ask searching and leading questions, and put a spin on every scrap of information you provide. This includes not only what you say and how you say it, but also how you appear and behave.

▶ **Judge:** You can't predict how each interviewer will react to you. We're all human, and different interviewers can interpret the same signal or piece of information in very different ways. However, it is possible to increase your chances of a positive judgement by putting lots of strong points forward and limiting anything that could be interpreted negatively.

▶ **Jury:** You are very much able to influence how you are viewed. Think about winding in any of the more extreme aspects of your personality, views, appearance and behaviour when job hunting. This is not about false pretences or compromising integrity; it's about not doing anything that could put an employer off you.

Your appearance

What you wear communicates strong messages, and this will almost certainly be the basis of the interviewer's first impression of you. That justifies giving it extra careful thought. You don't have to become anonymous; something unique about the way you look can help you be remembered above other candidates, but only if this is not so extreme as to be distracting. Compromise is the best approach.

For detailed guidelines on interview dress, please see **Chapter 19: What to wear.**

Your behaviour

Without wishing to make you paranoid, every action says something about you to an observer, so keep this in mind. The observation may start earlier than you think.

SOCIAL NETWORKING

In this age of digital networks, you can safely assume that an interviewer's assessment of your behaviour may well have begun before you even get to the interview.

Keep everything you can private, even if you don't think there's anything to worry about – why take the chance?

OUTSIDE

You might be seen as you walk from the car park to the door – and back again. Road rage has no place in the company car park, even if spaces are at a premium. Raising your middle finger at the person who poached your space shortly before you are interviewed by them (or their colleague) is not a great strategy.

Likewise, don't grind out a cigarette butt, adjust yourself in your trousers, hawk and spit, expel wind with gusto, swear loudly on your mobile or do anything you wouldn't do in front of the interviewer, anywhere within sight of the organization's premises.

Act as if the interview has begun the moment you walk into view.

INSIDE

Be polite and friendly with everyone you encounter whether outside the building, in reception or on the way to the interview room. You never know whose opinion of you might be sought and taken into account.

For more guidance on giving the right impression from start to finish, see **Chapter 21: How to appear/behave.**

Your communication

A skilled interviewer will use a variety of techniques to get you to reveal the kind of information they want to know about you. All their secret weapons can be turned to your advantage with sufficient preparation.

FACING QUESTIONS

An interviewer's first weapon is questions. Typically, they'll use a combination of open and closed questions. Open questions encourage you to supply information, such as 'Tell me a bit about your current job.' Closed questions have simpler, yes or no answers – 'Do you enjoy doing that?' Together, these two types of question help an interviewer to probe deeply into the areas they are most interested in.

> **Insight**
> The interviewer may appear to be leading the conversation, because they are asking the questions. However, unless you are in a fully structured interview with no room for deviation, you can still influence the direction of the interview through the answers you give.

Open questions
For the unprepared, open questions can be an invitation to mental block, or a licence to waffle with no clear point. Worse, there's a chance you might mention something you wanted to avoid. Like politicians, though, all interviewees should learn to love open questions: you can answer them however you choose and keep bringing the discussion back to the key points you want to make.

Closed questions
These can be far more challenging, as any politician who has faced Jeremy Paxman knows, but you don't have to stop at one-word answers. You can always bring in additional, positive information as well.

FACING SILENCE

The second, and probably most powerful, weapon of any good interviewer is silence. Never was the expression 'give someone enough rope to hang themselves' more apposite than during an interview.

If you impulsively tack comments onto the end of a well-answered question, you could contradict an earlier comment, raise an issue best kept quiet, or reduce the impact of your prepared answer.

Stick to the content of your prepared answers. Include your important points, then stop. There's nothing wrong with silence.

Insight

Silence preys upon our desire to please, in a situation where we're trying to make a good impression. You've just given your well-prepared answer, and the interviewer stays silent, raises an eyebrow, or (if really sneaky) says 'Oh?' or 'Go on.'

The desire to fill that silence can be enormous, but you need to resist.

YOUR FACE (AND BODY)

We all give out lots of non-verbal signals. Some you will be very aware of, others less so – but they are all important. If your non-verbal signals contradict what you are saying, they often carry more weight than your words. For example, if you explain how excellently you cope with pressurized situations, while your left foot is twitching, your fingers are tapping and your words are tumbling out at top speed, the interviewer will likely think you've overstated your ability.

Controlling your non-verbal communication

The main quality you want to project through non-verbal communication is confidence. You can learn to do this, even if you don't feel it inside.

Your posture, movements and how you speak (as opposed to what you say) also contribute to how you will be judged. You can't learn everything at once, but anyone can benefit from improving certain areas, so it pays to be aware of your own behaviour and how you should be aiming to present yourself.

Chapter 20: Getting into the zone – confidence tricks gives more details on developing positive non-verbal communication and how to portray confidence.

FOCAL POINTS

- Your interviewer will look at your appearance, behaviour and communication.

- Bland is not best, quirky can be memorable but extremism may count against you.

- Use social networks with care; control your settings and content.

- The interview starts as you approach the premises and finishes when you are out of sight.

- Avoid the temptation to fill every silence.

- Project confidence, even if you don't feel it.

- Don't let your face or body contradict what you're saying.

3

Different kinds of interview

In this chapter you will learn about:
- *the different interview formats*
- *the main types of interview*
- *the different stages of the interview process.*

Interviews can vary in three main ways:

1 **Format:** how many people are involved and where it takes place.
2 **Type:** based on the type or style of questioning. Rarely does an interview fall entirely into one type; it's more likely that the range of questions will span several types of interview.
3 **Stage:** there may be more than one interview stage. Two, three or more rounds of interviews may be called, depending on the nature and importance of the position and the number of short-listed candidates.

Classic interview formats

ONE-TO-ONE INTERVIEWS

This is a traditional format for many employers: it's just you and one interviewer. One-to-ones may take place face to face, by telephone, or via a video link/webcam.

Face-to-face interviews

The majority of interviews still take place in person; probably because, despite the expense of organizing them, most interviewers like to have a candidate directly in front of them in order to assess them properly.

Even if you begin with a telephone or video interview, it would be rare to be hired without having had at least one interview in person. You might find the prospect terrifying, but in almost every case it is far easier to communicate effectively in person.

Telephone interviews

These are often used as an easy, cost-effective way of screening a longer initial shortlist before inviting candidates to a face-to-face interview. While these can take place wherever you like, ideally you'll need a quiet location without any distractions.

Insight

Some companies even use automated telephone interviews as the first stage – this is supposed to help eliminate any possible bias. So don't be surprised if you call up and are speaking to a machine. If so, you're more likely to get multiple choice questions, but if you don't, make sure you speak clearly and slowly enough for your comments to register.

Telephone interviews sound like an easy option. You could do one from your bed, wearing your pyjamas, without even bothering to brush your hair, and no one would ever know; although taking too casual an attitude towards it could make you less careful with your answers. Take care what else you do during a telephone interview, too; however quiet you think you are, they'll be able to tell if you are eating, drinking or smoking while on the phone. No interviewer wants to hear the toilet flush as they thank you for your time!

Not being able to see the interviewer can make things harder – you can't see how they react to what you're telling them. Are they pleased, surprised, indifferent? This limited communication is rarely an advantage, which is why most employers use it only in the earliest stages of recruitment.

Video/webcam interviews

These are another good way of screening candidates, especially if the company is based some distance away or oversea and doesn't want the expense of transporting candidates to see them in person until they are more confident that you are what they're looking for. Depending on the equipment, this can be very similar to a face-to-face interview – provided you can see the interviewer's face clearly enough to read their expressions and you've got a live streaming image. There may be a time lag between their question and you hearing it, or your answer and their reaction. Their image, and yours, may freeze in various (usually uncomplimentary) poses if the video capability is poor – which can be quite off-putting.

Not every candidate will have access to a webcam; you may be asked to attend a location (for example their UK or regional office) where suitable equipment is available. If this happens, act as if your interview begins from the moment you approach the office – you may not be interviewed by the staff at this location but they could well be asked what they thought of you.

PANEL INTERVIEWS

This involves you and anything from two to ten interviewers. More is possible, but unlikely. More typically it would be three to five interviewers. Some organizations ensure panels always have an odd number of interviewers, so they can make a decisive vote about each candidate.

Panel interviews are commonly used for academic posts, medical positions and teaching roles, as there may be several people from the academic institution, the hospital team or the board of governors who need to be involved in making the decision. Instead of having sequential one-to-one interviews with each person in turn, they all question you, hear your answers to others' questions, and judge you on exactly the same performance.

Some corporate appointments may also have panel interviews, especially if it's for a senior executive position. That doesn't rule out the chance of having a panel interview if you're applying for a position that doesn't fall into one of these categories; some organizations might just like to see how you react to the situation.

The normal panel interview format is face to face, although it can also be done by video or web link. Panel interviews by telephone are thankfully very rare; co-ordinating questions from several interviewers becomes awkward over the phone, and it's quite disconcerting for an interviewee if you don't know who is asking each question.

Insight

Interviewers on a panel may ask questions seemingly independently of one another. Other times there will be an obvious leader. Ensure you look around the room as you give your answers, so that you include everyone on the panel.

GROUP INTERVIEWS

This is when you are grouped with any number of other candidates, and put together with one or more interviewers. In many cases the interviewer may not actually participate but will be more of an observer, there to assess everyone's performance at the same time. This type of interview can give insights into how you might behave as a team player, as a team leader, or with future clients.

Insight

The interviewer/assessor is not just interested in your ability in isolation, but in how you interact. They may wish to see how you position yourself within a team when given a choice; how you contribute to reaching a team objective; how you tackle a team negotiation; how you behave in a social setting. Don't turn inward or get too competitive: show that one of your individual talents is effective co-operation.

Group interviews may be overtly work-oriented, may appear more like a social event, or could be a mixture of the two. In either case, don't be fooled into assuming you know what they want and focusing only on that. In every work-oriented group interview, there will be plenty of elements of social interaction during meals and breaks. Equally, don't view an event that appears purely social as a brilliant freebie; take the opportunity to spend time with all the right people, and put yourself across professionally so they remember you and your skills rather than your ability to down beer and keep everyone amused.

Group interviews always take place in person because keen observation is required.

Work-based group interviews
These usually take place at the organization's premises or may be at a dedicated assessment centre. You'll typically face a series of work-based tasks over the course of one or even two days, either working together as one team or in smaller groups. Work-based tasks can include anything from creative thinking and problem-solving exercises to designing a new product, resurrecting a failing business or role-playing a negotiation.

Group interviews may include individual tests, too. Psychometric testing looks at personality and working styles, or they may focus on particular skills with IQ, time management, numeracy and language tests. One-to-one interviews with one or more people may also be scheduled throughout your time at an assessment centre.

Social-based group interviews

These could involve anything from a lunch or drinks reception to dinner out, or a challenge event designed to test teamwork skills. You might end up chatting over lunch in Manchester, planning a menu and cooking dinner for senior management in London, or raft building in Wales. And all the while you're sitting, standing (or swimming, if it didn't work out so well) shoulder to shoulder with the candidates you're competing against for the job.

Never be lulled into thinking that a social event or other activity has been laid on for your pure enjoyment, as a reward for simply applying. It might not always look like work on the surface, but it is; you still need to be demonstrating all the qualities and skills required for the job, whether that's selling yourself, schmoozing potential clients or networking effectively with a cross-section of the organization's staff. However, do try to *look* as if you are enjoying the proceedings.

Insight

Be extremely wary if asked for your opinion of other candidates in a group interview. Excessively competitive people who slate weaknesses in others don't make pleasant colleagues. Make positive observations about the group as a whole: how quickly you agreed roles, how well you brainstormed, how well you reached a joint goal. If pushed for individual feedback, say something positive but insignificant about each candidate: something not mentioned in the job criteria, so you're not selling them instead of yourself.

Common interview types

You may hear many different types or styles of interview mentioned. That could be structured versus unstructured, formal versus informal, general, behavioural, or competency; but trying to place an interview into a single category can be misleading. It's easy to fall into the trap of thinking that a particular interview type will only have a certain type of question.

When it comes to questions, most interviewers will have their personal favourites – those which tend to elicit the most useful information from candidates – but rarely will a skilled interviewer stick to just one type of question throughout an interview. Even the mildest-seeming interviewer may throw in some 'pressure tactic' questions, to see how you cope. When preparing, plan your answers and statements so that they are suitable for any style of question.

GENERAL QUESTIONS

As the name suggests, these are general requests for information or more detail. They can include questions like:

▶ 'Please can you start by telling me a bit about yourself?'
▶ 'What can you offer our company?'
▶ 'Outline your sales successes to date.'
▶ 'What are the key career moves you've made since starting work?'

These queries tend to be quite straightforward and are designed to get detail or insight beyond your CV. The expected answer is usually based on your employment history and relevant experience, although this is a golden opportunity to bring in all of the key points you'd like to make.

Warm up fast

General questions are often used purely as a warm-up to get the conversation going. That doesn't mean you should treat them as less important: they will shape the initial impression you make.

The interviewer may also use them as a basis for assessing your communication skills – whether you can summarize and present relevant information clearly and concisely.

These questions may also be a starting point for probing in more depth how well you've performed for previous organizations, in the hope that you will bring similar value to your next employer.

False sense of security

General questions may sound like the easiest type to answer, but for that very reason they should take the most preparation. There is no excuse for wasting an opportunity to present a great snapshot of yourself, taken from whichever angle you think is best. Initial impressions may have been formed before you're even asked the first question, but you can guarantee your early answers will also carry a lot of weight.

Can you answer all of the most common questions, clearly and concisely, in a minute or less? Once you can, do still pause and think before answering so that you come across as spontaneous and not too rehearsed.

BEHAVIOURAL (OR COMPETENCY) QUESTIONS

With these, the interviewer is interested in your past performance as a way of predicting your future performance. They don't just want to find out *what* you did for Bleeding Radiators Ltd, they want to know *how* you did it – what skills you used to succeed. By understanding how you have acted in past work situations, they hope to gain more of an insight into how you might perform if you came to work for their company.

Typical questions start with:

▶ 'Tell me about a time when you…'
▶ 'Describe a situation where you…'
▶ 'Can you give me an example of when…'

Transferable skills

The real beauty of behavioural or competency questioning is that it allows an interviewer to focus on the transferable skills and qualities you have, rather than being limited to the context in which you've used your skills. This can help to widen the recruitment net, which is important for employers who want the biggest possible pool of talent to choose from. It also means you can argue that your limited experience in this field is less of a hindrance.

For example, it starts to matter less whether you have 'computer sales experience', and more that you have a combination of 'selling skills' and the 'ability to learn technical information quickly, and explain it in a simple way'. This combination of skills could be developed and shown in a number of different ways, not only through proven success in a computer sales job.

Varied experience

The competency style of interviewing means you can short-list people with quite differing levels of industry- or job-related experience, and compare them on a fairly equal footing, by asking them all exactly the same behavioural questions. The earlier question about working as part of a successful team might just as easily be answered using an example from team sports, volunteering or work experience as it might by giving an example from recent employment – which means school leavers and recent graduates need not be at a disadvantage.

Lots of examples

Does showing a skill in one environment mean you'll be able to apply it successfully in other circumstances? A single, isolated behavioural or competency question can't reliably determine this. Ideally you should be asked to provide more than one example of each skill, but if your interviewer doesn't ask, there's nothing wrong with volunteering a second example. The more evidence you indicate for each of your skills/ competencies, the more likely the interviewer is to build an impression of you as an adaptable person whose skills could benefit any employer. Preparing sufficient 'proof' of every skill you claim to have (even if you don't end up discussing all of it) is worth spending time on.

FORMAL OR STRUCTURED INTERVIEWS

Behavioural- or competency-based interviews may sometimes be called 'formal' or 'structured' interviews. This simply means that the questions (and maybe even the order of questioning) will be exactly the same for every single candidate. The idea behind it is that all candidates, whatever their level of experience, will have an opportunity to impress with their skills, no matter how, where or when these skills have been developed.

'Unstructured' or 'informal' interviews may be used to describe those where the questions are not all pre-set; each candidate's interview can go in a different direction, driven by the answers the candidate gives and how the interviewer chooses to pursue any avenues that open up.

PRESSURE INTERVIEWS

These are rarely advertised as such in advance, but some people see these as a distinct type of interview. The idea behind them is to ask you questions that are considered more challenging – either because of what they are asking about, or the way in which they are phrased. Some interviewers will change their whole demeanour, becoming quite negative, provocative or even rude, just to put you on the spot and see how you cope.

More challenging questions are covered in Chapters 12 to 16. **Chapter 24: Troubleshooting** discusses how to deal with difficult interviewers.

Preparation

Whether an interview is competency-based, structured or otherwise shouldn't affect how you prepare. Knowing that every other candidate will get the exact same questions – or that they won't – doesn't really help.

Insight

Many employers use interview definitions quite loosely: don't breathe a sigh of relief if you are invited to an 'informal interview over lunch' and not bother preparing so much. Every interview should be treated with the same level of respect and preparation; no interview label or location can predict how gently or harshly you may be questioned.

Behavioural questioning may also be used to give the interviewer some insight into your working style, and whether you'd be easy or impossible to manage. Interviewers may also drift into hypothetical questions – 'What would you do if...?' – to see how you'd be likely to deal with something you've had little or no experience of.

The best way to handle any type of question is to make sure it doesn't take you completely by surprise, which means planning as many answers as possible before you get there.

See Chapters 10 to 16 for the most common questions, different types of question, and a guide to preparing your answers to these.

Interview stages

There aren't any hard-and-fast rules about what will happen at each interview stage, or how many stages or rounds of interviews there might be. Every organization and each vacancy will differ. This is simply an outline as to what you could expect, and why.

TESTING

This can happen at any stage of interview, but you will normally be warned to expect it. Note carefully whether any presentations, psychometric tests, IQ tests, numeracy tests or other types of exercise are likely on the day. If you attend an assessment centre, it is highly likely you will be asked to take part in additional exercises of some kind.

Insight

Testing is beyond the scope of this book, but look up any test you are not familiar with, and practise any you know you'll be set. Your results are not fixed by your personality or intellect – everyone can benefit from practising IQ test questions, for example.

There are many books about IQ, psychometric and numeracy tests, with examples. There's also plenty of information online.

Make sure you prepare any presentations or other tasks well in advance of the interview; there's no excuse for prepared work not being perfectly polished and practised. Don't forget to bring all your prepared work on the day, along with any props you need.

FIRST INTERVIEWS

Obviously at this stage the number of candidates is highest and recruiters want to short-list preferred candidates as quickly and as cost-effectively as possible. You might be offered a job on the basis of just one interview, although many organizations will hold several rounds.

Smaller organizations

If you're applying to join a smaller organization, such as a local business or shop, the chances are you'll be interviewed by the recruiting manager you'll be working for, or even the owner themselves. They'll be less likely to use an agency (unless it's for temporary work) and may not have a personnel department as such.

This means they should understand clearly the role you are applying for, and could make the decision to hire you without having to consult anyone else.

Larger organizations

Short, basic 'screening' interviews may be done over the phone rather than face to face if there are lots of applicants who appear to be suitable. In larger organizations these may even be automated, as the questions are normally simple and straightforward.

Initial interviews may also be conducted by a recruitment agency rather than the employer. Even if the employer does carry out the first round of interviews themselves, these will often be done by someone from the personnel or human resources (HR) department, rather than the recruiting manager.

What to mention

The focus should be on putting across how well you meet their job description, with plenty of supporting examples of the skills and experience you claim to have. You should also make it clear that you've done your research on the company and why you are really interested in this opportunity.

What to avoid

As a guideline, don't volunteer any salary information at first interview. Recruitment agencies will usually ask what you're on and what you might expect/hope for, and HR people often will for the record, but if the person opposite you doesn't ask, don't raise the subject yourself. In round one, the focus should be on demonstrating your suitability and commitment to this role and this employer, not on what you want to get out of it.

Your negotiating position may be stronger if a prospective employer doesn't know your salary until they've decided they want to hire you, but don't duck the issue if they ask outright. The classic 'If you're making me an offer, then I'd be more than happy to discuss details of my remuneration,' can seem arrogant unless it's a very senior position.

Vagueness is more acceptable when talking about your salary expectations: in this case being less specific can help avoid pricing yourself out of a job too early in the process.

SECOND/LATER INTERVIEWS

This might be with the same interviewer from the first round or someone new.

Smaller organizations

This could be with the same person, following up in more detail on issues raised by your first interview. The interviewer will usually have seen all the other candidates by now, so some of the questions could be quite specific, based on information they have given. The second interview could also be with someone more senior.

Larger organizations

If round one was with an agency, round two is when you'd expect to see a face from the employer side. If you saw someone from HR in the first round, you might expect to gain access this time to someone from the department that's recruiting. There are no guarantees, though. You might be invited in just for some psychometric testing, with little in the way of any follow-up interview until those results are analysed.

As before, the best approach is to know (or find out) who is doing the interviewing and to think about what they're likely to be interested in. The closer to the actual job the interviewer is, the more likely they will want to know relevant details about your experience, skills, and how you can bring value to the job. Industry jargon is more likely to be understood, so questions and answers may be more technical in nature.

Insight

If you are told (or can find out) the interviewer's name before you come in, try an Internet search on their name and company. Sites like LinkedIn can be great sources of relevant business information and give you clues as to their age, background, how long they've been with the company and other areas of interest. Finding common ground between yourself and your interviewer – if used subtly – can be very useful.

As with earlier stages of interview, the best rule is to ask as many questions as you like about the job, the team and the organization, but never raise the subject of salary yourself.

FINAL INTERVIEWS

Towards the end of the process there may only be you and a couple of other candidates left. Most organizations will keep at least three or four people in the final round of discussions in case their first-choice candidate turns down their offer of a job.

As part of your final interview stage, you may have some further discussions with HR. They are usually quite interested in your salary, your salary or package expectations, and anything else that motivates you. Their aim is to be sure that, if they reach the point of making you a formal offer, you are likely to accept it. They may at this stage also ask you for references.

You could also expect to be interviewed by the manager you would be working for, especially if you haven't met them yet, and possibly also their boss or the head of department. If you're going for a role with a larger company that encourages internal progression through different departments, or there are several vacancies up for grabs, you could end up being interviewed by various managers.

Final-stage interviews may take place in isolation, or may be sometimes combined with other activities such as group tasks in an assessment centre.

CLOSING THE DEAL

Whatever the interview stage – but particularly if you know it's the final round and therefore decision time – if you're being interviewed by the decision-making manager then always try to close the deal before the interview finishes: ask for the job. It shows you want it, for starters, and that you are not afraid to ask for what you want.

Even if you're told a decision can't be made yet, asking the question will offer you a great opportunity to ask for some feedback, and this can help you to address any remaining concerns or negative perceptions the interviewer has. At best you could walk out with a provisional offer of a job, even if you have to wait to talk about salary – which, of course, you won't mention first.

FOCAL POINTS

- Approach every interview or task with equal respect, however informal it may seem.

- Most interviewers rely on a mixture of question types, not just one kind.

- Nothing should surprise the truly well prepared.

- Know who is interviewing you and their likely level of knowledge.

- Always keep in mind the key points you want the interviewer to know about you.

- Never bring up the issue of salary yourself.

- Ask for the job – you have little to lose and lots to gain.

Part two
Preparation

4

Know yourself

In this chapter you will learn about:
- *the importance of thinking through your motivation for going for a particular job*
- *working out a broader career path into which this job may fit*
- *developing a generic CV*
- *controlling your image on networking sites such as Facebook and LinkedIn.*

From Part one, you should have a fairly good idea what to expect from the interview you've been invited for. This is where you start to prepare in detail.

A great way to prepare is by creating an interview crib sheet. Your crib sheet will contain all the relevant information you want the interviewer to know about you. It will be phrased in a clear, concise way, and will include some prepared statements and lots of answers to potential questions.

Once you've written one crib sheet, you'll find you can quite easily adapt it for other interviews. You may need to delete some things, or add new parts, depending on the skills and experience each job advert asks for and any experience you've gained in the meantime, but you'll find it gets quicker to write every time you revisit it.

Preparing for an interview means knowing what you're going to say. This means making sure that you...

▶ know yourself
▶ know the role
▶ know the organization

- ▶ know the interviewer
- ▶ know the questions.

In this chapter we'll deal with the first of these. You can't convince an employer that you're suitable for a job and that you really want it, until *you* know why. Taking the time to think this through will prove valuable for your next interview and for many more in future.

Why apply?

Why do people apply for the jobs they do? It might be in desperation, perhaps after losing your job; falling out with your manager; being told you are going to be made redundant or feeling frustrated with your current work. Maybe you've just left school or university. Maybe you've been in the same job for years and want to see what you're worth in the marketplace. You might need a stronger negotiating position in order to get a pay rise from your current employer; or you might just like reassurance that your current job isn't quite so terrible after all. Sometimes it can be prompted by sheer boredom; other times you might spy a job advert in the paper for an opportunity you'd never considered but really like the sound of. Maybe chance seats you next to someone who's hiring, and they like you and encourage you to apply. There are also people who plan their careers carefully and only apply for the jobs they know will get them to where they want to be; most of us, however, aren't as organized as this.

Whatever your current motivation and whatever career path you've taken to reach this point, planned or otherwise, you can't really start preparing for any interview until you've sat down and taken a bit of time to think about what you're doing here, and why. Even if you didn't have this chat with yourself before writing your CV and posting your application, you really do need to have it now.

Questions to ask yourself

Try writing short, honest answers to the following questions: this is for your use only. Short is important, because it will make your task easier when you need to come back to these answers. Honest is important, because it will help you craft your story and limit any weak spots. You won't share any of this with an employer until everything counts for you, not against you.

QUESTION 1: WHAT DO YOU WANT FROM YOUR NEXT JOB?

This might be absolutely anything: greater job security, more enjoyment or satisfaction, some management responsibility, better training opportunities, building industry experience, earning commission, gaining formal qualifications, developing certain skills, shorter hours, more overtime, earning more money, less stress, more holidays, improving your social life, huge bonuses, less travel/time away from home, flexible working hours, a company car, getting a step closer to being a millionaire, going part time, learning a language, making friends, working in your favourite industry, having a job share, being more creative, working abroad, being more people-oriented, making an impact on the world around you, etc.

Is there more than one path that could get you what you want? Are there several types of job you could (or should) be applying for which might help you achieve the same result, or get closer to it? Note them all down.

Insight

If you're really not sure about this step, it may make sense to stop applying for jobs until you do. Otherwise, you'll just end up back on the market again in no time. If you're applying for jobs because you're under time pressure and this can't wait, jot down a few things you like the sound of most, and continue with those in mind.

QUESTION 2: WHY DO YOU WANT THIS?

You've hopefully been honest in answering the first question. For now, ignore any personal or reward-based items such as more money or time off, and focus on any aspects that are purely related to career development. This could include developing skills, building experience, seeking new challenges, gaining relevant qualifications, learning new languages, etc. What's your ultimate career goal? Do you even have one? Where are the things you gain from this new job supposed to take you next? And what could be the step after that?

Even if you don't have a firm idea of your potential career path – maybe it's your first job and you don't really know where you want to head yet, perhaps there are too many options for you to choose just one, or maybe you don't care as long as you're getting paid – you still need to come up with a plausible-sounding plan. Aimless wandering until you find a job you like, or an employer that'll have you, isn't a brilliant career strategy. Admitting that this is what you're doing is unlikely to encourage an employer to help you get there, either.

Thinking up a plausible goal, and a strategy for getting there, is not dishonest. It will help to give your job hunt a framework, and this means you'll be able to add logic, consistency and depth to your interview answers.

QUESTION 3: WHO DO YOU WANT TO GET THIS FROM?

What's the most important thing about any future employer? Is it their way of doing business, market-leading position, ethical reputation, innovative approach to business, prestige status, international opportunities, investment in staff, risk-taking culture, rapid growth, great working atmosphere or the simple fact that they are unlikely to go belly up and you won't be redundant again?

Select from the above, or decide on whatever is most important to you – the key is that it *is* important to you. It will all form part of your story.

QUESTION 4: WHAT CAN YOU OFFER THEM IN RETURN?

If you've already written an application form or CV, use this as your starting point. If you have followed the Teach Yourself guide on CV writing (Julie Gray, *Get That Job with the Right CV*), refer to your generic CV for this section: you will have already done most, if not all, of the work when you created this document.

Without a particular vacancy in mind, or referring to any job adverts, list all of your skills, qualities, experience and knowledge. Against each item, note down two or three examples that prove you do indeed possess each one.

Insight

All examples or 'proofs' should be SHORT-listed. That means they need to be:

▶ Short
▶ Honest
▶ Outcome-driven (what benefit did you create?)
▶ Realistic (i.e. believable)
▶ Transferable (to other situations)

For more detail on SHORT-listing, read *Get That Job with the Right CV*.

Next, look at any obvious skills or experience you may be lacking, and think about whether you can gain that during your next job or whether it's something you could focus on sorting out for yourself.

Lastly, look at what you think are the major weaknesses in your CV: experience you don't yet have, incomplete qualifications, unexplained absences, or gaps in employment. All of these could be viewed negatively by an interviewer and you'll often need to go over these areas in detail. It helps if you can prepare for this by using honest spin: taking any situation, however poor, and finding a way to develop it into a positive story. Provided it's honest, it will help you to be far more upbeat and confident when going into interview.

Social networks

It's worth repeating the warning. What's forgotten by you in moments, the Internet may hang onto for years. And if you've ever uploaded a photo onto Facebook, that company's policy on copyright could mean that it comes back to haunt you even after you've taken it down.

If there is (or could be) anything 'out there' on a social networking site like Facebook, MySpace, Twitter, Bebo, or even a blog, that might not hold a positive light to your career or personal integrity – especially if you were just a teeny bit drunk when you posted it – then sort it out now, if you can. Even if you didn't upload something yourself, you might have been tagged in a few too many photos of drunken nights out.

Another issue sites like Facebook or Twitter can raise with employers is just how much time you spend on social networks when you should be working. If your status updates come in every few minutes during a working day, it doesn't show much commitment to your current job.

Check, double-check, increase your privacy settings, edit, remove, do whatever you have to, but try to dissociate yourself from anything that isn't positive for your image. If you don't deal with your Facebook faux pas, none of your evidence may overcome your potential employer's perception of you after a quick web search. Keep this in mind at the very start of any job application; otherwise on interview day (if you ever get that far) it could lead to some very awkward questions.

Insight

If there's anything sordid about you online, and getting a job is important to you, you could consider the bold step of deleting your social networking account. You can always resuscitate it later, after you get the job, and be more careful from then on.

If you're just starting your career, think about cleaning up your social networking and using it differently. Keep anything controversial for direct messaging or texts, don't post publicly anything that could backfire – and ask friends to respect you and do the same.

Business networks

Don't forget LinkedIn, or any similar networks of business contacts that you may belong to. While less likely to cause embarrassment than social networks, they are commonly checked by recruiters and therefore should at least be kept up to date. Ideally, tweak your profile to be relevant to the industry or employer you are applying to.

FOCAL POINTS

- However you got here, make it look like it makes sense to you.

- Be clear what you want out of work in general.

- Decide what you want from your next job.

- Ask yourself how this next job will further your career.

- Understand what you can offer an employer.

- Prove your claims with SHORT-listed examples.

- Be aware of the less positive parts of your CV.

- Use honest spin to address your weaker points.

- Don't let yourself down by letting your guard down on social networks.

- Keep your business network profile up to date and relevant.

5

Know the role

In this chapter you will learn that:
- *it's crucial to research the nature of the job you're applying for thoroughly*
- *you must have a clear idea both of what you can bring to the role and what you can take from it.*

To prove you really want the job, you need to know *why* you really want the job. You can't know that unless you know exactly what it involves, so research, research, research.

To make your research focused and effective, try asking yourself the following four questions. If you can answer each in less than one minute, you'll be well on your way to convincing an interviewer that you're the right person for this job.

QUESTION 1: WHAT KIND OF ACTIVITIES DOES THIS JOB INVOLVE?

Check the job ad and job description supplied, or try to find one online. Failing that, find descriptions for similar-sounding roles in other companies and make an educated guess as to what might be involved in this one.

QUESTION 2: HOW DOES THIS ROLE IMPACT/BENEFIT THE COMPANY?

Look at what you'd be doing and at the company's overall business objectives (read whatever information they've sent you and/or search online for more details).

Then, make some assumptions about how you, in this role, could help the company achieve its targets or objectives. It can be difficult to do this when you're looking at an entry-level role, but you can still have some appreciation of the part you might play.

For example, if you're a supermarket shelf stacker, your job is basically to keep products available for shoppers to buy, displayed nicely on the shelves. Doing this well means customers should spend more in the shop. Untidy shelves with out-of-stock items means losing sales when customers can't find what they want. They might even start shopping elsewhere if they get annoyed with products always being unavailable. So, as a successful shelf stacker, you could contribute to the store's sales (and profitability), and to the supermarket chain's overall market share.

If you're a receptionist, your job is to act as the entry point for everyone contacting the company – in person, by phone, by fax or even by email. If you handle all incoming contact quickly and helpfully, passing them to the appropriate departments without delay, then people contacting the company will find it friendly and professional and will be more likely to return with future business. A great receptionist can contribute to positive company performance.

Insight

If you're finding it hard to answer this question, or if you haven't got any work experience, don't be afraid to get help. Try asking friends, family, or anyone around you who might be able to help you understand or work out where you would fit in.

QUESTION 3: WHY WOULD YOU BE GOOD AT THIS JOB?

Write a short summary statement about why your particular combination of skills and experience is so well suited to this role. Be as specific as possible – ensure you mention all the key criteria the job advert mentions, plus anything else you feel would be an advantage.

Once you have written down the detail about what the role entails, you'll be able to think ahead to how you might handle each specific area, and what you would potentially focus on or aim to improve if you did get the job. Would you work more accurately because of your experience, motivate people better because of your management skills, or speed up the process because of your problem-solving ability?

QUESTION 4: WHY DO YOU WANT TO DO THIS JOB?

Again, this should be a summary statement of no more than a
minute. First, you want to add value to the company, so you could
start by summarizing your answer to question 3. Mention briefly the
desirable skills/qualities you could bring to the role that would enable
you to do it really well and enjoy it.

Secondly, you want to get something out of it yourself. Talk about
which aspects of your skills and experience you would be able to
develop and broaden while doing this job.

It's always appreciated if you can see this two-way benefit working
well in the long term, not just for the coming year. Keep the scope
of your statement wide enough to include what you enjoy (or
would enjoy) most about doing this kind of role, and the sort of
opportunities you hope it could lead to in future.

FOCAL POINTS

- You can't genuinely want a role that you don't understand – so find out about it.

- Research is key to understanding what the job involves.

- Know how your strengths will help you to do this role well.

- Think about how you would improve performance if you did get the job.

- Understand what the job could give you professionally, i.e. development and training.

- Work out other roles that this job could help to prepare you for.

6

Know the organization

In this chapter you will learn that:
- *it's vital to research as much as you can about the organization to which you are applying*
- *you can use a variety of resources to find out information*
- *you should be prepared to display what you have learned at the interview.*

It's relatively easy to get basic information about a job vacancy – the basics are normally there in black and white in the job advert. To understand enough about the organization behind the vacancy, you will need to do some in-depth research.

Hopefully you applied with a targeted CV, which means you'll have done your company research already. If you haven't, consider it your essential next step. You'd be surprised how many people don't bother with this stage, or skimp on it, even when they're aiming for a high-profile job.

Insight

If you don't believe research can make a difference, think about the popular BBC series *The Apprentice*. This has been running for several years now, so you'd think candidates should know what to expect, yet there are *still* those who make it as far as the interview round with only a faint idea of Lord Sugar's businesses and what they do. However positive their performance, that round is usually their last.

Why research?

There's really no excuse for not researching the organization you're applying to. Would you commit to buying a house to live in without knowing what kind of area it was in, or how many bedrooms it had, or without viewing it at least once? Yet you may consider applying for a job that you will spend most of your waking hours doing, which will have a significant impact on your state of mind, the earnings from which will pay for wherever you live, without so much as an interested glance? Pretend you are seeking a house, not a job: apply the same level of diligence to researching any company you'd consider joining.

Use your consultant

If a recruitment agency has been appointed to fill the vacancy you are interested in, you can tap into their client knowledge to find out some of the basic detail that you should know about any prospective employer. Recruitment agencies may also have useful 'inside' information that may be less easy to find online or through other routes – this is particularly true of department-level information.

This is no substitute for your own research, though; after all, the recruitment consultant will be telling this information to anyone who asks. They will also be doing their best to sell the company and the opportunity to you, because if you don't accept the job offer, they won't earn their commission.

Basic research questions

When you're researching a company online it's very easy to get sidetracked, which is not ideal if you have an interview in a matter of days or even hours. Unless time is not an issue, try focusing your research to answer a few basic questions about the organization:

- ▶ What products or services does it offer?
- ▶ Where and to whom does it market/sell its products or services?
- ▶ What sort of reputation does it have – market leader, innovative, fast-growing?
- ▶ Is it part of a bigger company and if so, which (and what does it do)?
- ▶ Which other companies does this one compete with?
- ▶ What's happened recently?
- ▶ What are its overall objectives and how might your role contribute to those?

Research sources

By far the best way to research an organization is using the Internet. Google their website first, to see how much you can find out on their main pages, before following any links. You should be able to find information about company performance, objectives and working philosophy on their main site, and even be able to look up key directors. This can be handy if you're being interviewed by a member of the senior management team. Smaller companies without a website of their own may still appear in online news items or directories. However, depending on the nature of their business, it might pay to be a little cautious about your prospects within a company that has zero web presence.

Once you know the names of the organization's products or services, you can Google those separately to uncover anything from retail prices to customer reviews, from competing products (make a note of who their competitors are) to upcoming launches.

Companies that are owned by larger corporations can often be identified from product packaging, or from checking the bottom of a web page. Otherwise Google something like 'Which company owns Elusive Details plc?'

You can find some interesting insights into companies from former employees, in blogs, archives and recent news articles, and from trade partners (suppliers or customers). Googling any of these can add to the overall picture.

LIBRARY

If you don't have Internet access at home, try your local library as you may be able to search online from there. Failing that, ask a librarian for help to research the organization you're interested in; you'd be surprised how much information some libraries hold, and the librarian is always your best and quickest route to finding it all.

CONTACTS

You can also try asking around; if you follow your network of family, friends and business associates far enough, you should stumble across someone who knows someone who works or did work for the organization. You can ask them all sorts of questions about the company's ethos, culture, etc., although bear in mind responses can be quite subjective and will depend on the person's individual experiences.

Further research questions

If you have a little more time, you could also look into these areas:

- ▶ What future plans does the company have and how might that affect your role?
- ▶ How does the company operate, what is the culture like?
- ▶ How well does it (and its products/services) perform compared to the competition?
- ▶ Are its competitors also hiring in this area? Get familiar with their job ads, too.
- ▶ Would working for this company be better than working for a competitor? Why?
- ▶ Is the role new or existing? If existing, why did the previous job holder leave?

Interesting research questions

Finally, if you have the luxury of even more time, or if you know much of the above already, you could also dig around for answers to the following:

- ▶ What industry/marketplace trends might be relevant to the organization?
- ▶ Is there any future legislation coming that will have an impact on the organization?
- ▶ How has the company performed this past year (this could be in general, in the marketplace, or against its stated objectives)?
- ▶ How is the company rated by its employees (existing and former, although bear in mind each group may have a different agenda)?

Insight

For a more senior role, it can be worthwhile to perform a SWOT analysis. Consider the organization's Strengths, Weaknesses, Opportunities and Threats, and then think about how you would build on, improve on, capitalize on and neutralize them respectively. If you can relate this specifically to your job, so much the better.

Why do more than the minimum?

Augmenting your research is not just suggested as a way of filling your time before you go for your interview. The more you know about the organization you want to join, the more convincing you will be when you say you're keen on the job, and the greater the edge you will have over other candidates. If you're up against someone with more experience or more highly developed skills than you, this is one way you can really stand out. (This particularly applies, but is not limited to, school leavers and graduates.) If you have the time, spend it wisely.

What to do with your research

Once you have completed all your research, it's time to learn the key points by heart. You could be quizzed in detail if you claim to know a lot about the company, so be prepared.

After you have learned as much as you can, condense the highlights into a one-minute statement. This will come in handy later when you're preparing answers to relevant questions, including some of the most common questions – discussed in **Chapter 10: The 15 most common questions.**

FOCAL POINTS

- Research should be the first stage of any application, before you even write your CV.

- Attending an interview without research can undermine even the strongest candidate.

- Use your recruitment consultant, the Internet, local libraries and all your contacts.

- Knowing the basics is essential but that won't give you the edge over others.

- Taking time to understand an organization and its challenges will win you points.

- Claiming you've carried out research is no good, you must prove it – learn it by heart.

- Show you're a good communicator by preparing a summary of what you know.

7

Know the interviewer

In this chapter you will learn:
- *finding out as much as you can about your interviewer(s) can be a vital tool in your interview*
- *how you may be able to use shared interests or experience to your advantage.*

Here you don't need in-depth knowledge, like the interviewer's favourite colour or whether they take two sugars in their tea, but an understanding of who they are and what role they do in the organization can be really helpful. Even just their job title is better than nothing.

If you are going via a recruitment agency, your consultant should be worth their weight in gold at this point. You can ask them anything and everything you'd like to know about your interviewer, including their background, responsibilities and what they are like as a person.

Insight
Don't feel you can be lazy if you can tap a recruitment consultant for information: you'll actually have to work harder to find things that work to your advantage, as the other candidates will all have access to the same source. Anything you find out over and above the norm (whether it's from the consultant or from other sources) could give you the edge you're looking for.

What should you know?

The kinds of questions you should aim to answer about your interviewer include:

WHO ARE THEY, WHAT DO THEY DO AND WHAT IS THEIR WORK HISTORY?

▶ Do they work in HR, or the department you would be joining? Is their main interest in you as a potential company employee or as a member of their team?

▶ Are they senior enough to have a 'bio' on the company website? If so, check it out and see how much of their background is mentioned.

▶ Do they have a LinkedIn or other networking web page? If so, see if they've published their CV so that you can check out their background and career history.

You never know, you might find something in common with the interviewer: a love of new music; having worked for the same company in the past; a shared academic background. Basic psychology dictates that, whether we're conscious of it or not, we're drawn to people who are similar to us; if you have anything in common with the interviewer, make sure you bring up the subject at some point during the interview.

WHAT LEVEL OF DECISION MAKER ARE THEY?

▶ Can this person actually offer you the job, or are they just screening candidates and/or making a recommendation to the hiring manager?

Don't underestimate 'screeners': they may not be able to offer you the job but they can certainly determine whether you're in with a shout. If they can offer you the job – and especially if it's a sales-oriented role – make sure to ask for the job as soon as there's an opportunity to.

WHAT KIND OF QUESTIONS MIGHT THEY BE LIKELY TO ASK?

HR questions are likely (but not guaranteed) to be more general – checking the details of your CV, career motivations, reasons for joining the company. Line manager questions will probably be more job-oriented; you may be asked for proof of job-specific skills, or asked to give your thoughts on an issue that is relevant to the role.

Anyone could ask you about anything, which is why it's good to prepare for all possibilities when planning your answers. Keep your audience in mind, though: an HR person may not react well to (or be impressed by, or possibly even understand) job-specific jargon, whereas a line manager might invite it or expect it.

WHAT KIND OF PERSON ARE THEY AND HOW DO THEY LIKE TO INTERVIEW?

▶ Are they expressive, friendly and talkative?
▶ Are they quieter, more inscrutable, harder to read, formal?
▶ Do they like to use pressure tactics?
▶ What types of question might they favour?

It can really help to know about these aspects of the interviewer's approach: if you're getting a stony face from someone who is normally open and friendly, then perhaps what you're saying isn't being well received. Whereas a stony face from someone you're expecting one from is far less off-putting.

Using your insights

Once you've found out as much as you can about the interviewer, make sure you put it to good use. Note down any points that could influence how you prepare your answers and statements. If they speak little themselves and are known to appreciate brevity in others, try working up shorter-than-usual answers. If they like detail, be sure to include significant or relevant details when giving examples of your skills. Conversely, if they are a 'big picture' person, stick to your outline version when describing any experiences.

FOCAL POINTS

- Knowing your audience is essential if you want to target your answers properly.

- The interviewer's job should shape how much or how little jargon you can safely use.

- Understanding the interviewer's preferences can help you anticipate questions.

- Insights into the interviewer's personality will help you understand their feedback signals.

- Try to mention anything you share with the interviewer: similarity is positive.

- Use your insights to shape your prepared answers; otherwise it's a wasted effort.

8

....

Know the questions

In this chapter you will learn about:
- *the broad categories of interview questions*
- *how the weight given to each is likely to change at different points in your career*
- *the importance of tailoring answers to each interview situation.*

This is the chapter that everyone rushes to, in the hope of some miracle answers that no other candidate will have. That's not really the focus of this section; it's more of a guide to get you to think about the most likely questions you could face, and help you to avoid pitfalls when preparing your unique responses.

If this book could give you perfect answers, that would be little, if any, advantage in itself. However fantastic those answers might be, they would be widely available for anyone else to read, rehearse and recite. No book can offer every reader a perfect answer anyway, because every person and interview is unique.

Far more valuable than reciting obviously stock answers, is learning how to tackle questions yourself and preparing and rehearsing answers that show you in the best possible light.

Question categories

Questions that you may be asked tend to fall into one of the following categories:

- ▶ small talk
- ▶ education
- ▶ work experience

- ▶ skills/behaviours/competencies
- ▶ personality/personal qualities
- ▶ preferences/working style
- ▶ motivation/commitment/ambitions
- ▶ interests.

You can predict to some extent which ones an interviewer is most likely to focus on.

Likely lines of questioning

All interviews will require you to indulge in some level of small talk, whether it's with the receptionist, other candidates, the interviewer's PA or the interviewer themselves. The relative weights given to other lines of questioning will vary according to factors such as your level of experience.

SCHOOL LEAVERS OR GRADUATES

You can normally expect the majority of questions to be about your education, your interests, and any work or volunteering experience you may have. Questions about personal qualities and competencies will be more likely as you may not have any work experience to draw upon. Hypothetical questions could be used to ask you about how you might react in a work situation.

EARLY CAREER

Once you've been working for two or three years, you could still be asked about your education in some detail – and especially if the course content is relevant to the job you're going for. However, your recent work history and newly developed skills are likely to be the main focus of any questions.

EXPERIENCED EMPLOYEES

After working for ten or more years, it's unlikely you'll face any questions about your education – unless a career change means it becomes relevant again. Your work experience, professional development and competencies will carry far more weight than academic qualifications, unless you're continuing to study and they are relevant to your job.

Career intentions, ambitions and future plans will be of interest to every employer, no matter at what stage your career is currently. The fact that you've given the topic consideration and are actively pursuing a goal will count in your favour.

Interests or hobbies you pursue outside work may also be of interest – it really depends on the interviewer. Many interviewers use this section of your CV as an ice breaker, just to get you talking freely and over any initial nerves. Others use it to find out what sort of a person you are – adventurous, a risk taker, independent, conservative, team-oriented? Skilled interviewers will often use questions about hobbies as a benchmark, to see how you are when you talk about something you're enthusiastic about. They can then compare this with how you seem when you talk about your past work, or the job opportunity you're going for.

Insight

Ensure that you put as much effort into planning answers about your interests as you do for any other question category; every topic, every answer, is a chance to reinforce the key points you want to make.

Wrong answer, or wasted opportunity?

In most cases, the biggest issue you're likely to have with a question is not that you answer it 'wrongly', but that you won't make the very most of it. You have a limited number of questions in an interview, and each offers you a chance to shine. Miss a chance, and you won't get it back again.

The answers to every question should be shaped by you, so that you leave the interviewer knowing all your relevant strengths and what you can offer the company. This means preparing all your answers well in advance. Sitting in front of an interviewer is not the ideal place to be thinking about a particular question for the very first time.

Insight

If you plan your answers properly, the answer you give to one question in one interview may be very different from your response to an identical question in another interview. Every job advert asks for different things, so the points you need to emphasize should differ for each interview. Perhaps not by much, but they should change.

FOCAL POINTS

- Most questions fall into one of eight main categories.

- How long you've been working determines what's of most interest to the interviewer.

- Never waste a chance to mention your main selling points, whatever the question.

- Borrowed answers impress no one; plan out your own unique responses.

- Tailor your answers to each job opportunity.

9

Know how to answer

In this chapter you will learn about:
- *a specific and a general approach to answering interview questions*
- *how to plan, refine and condense your answers.*

If you prepare properly for an interview, you will feel far more confident than if you don't. It's as if you're going into an exam knowing all the answers because you found out the questions in advance. There is no guarantee the wording on the question paper won't change a little, and you might find a couple of new questions added – but in essence, all the foundations will be there.

The confidence you gain from being well prepared will go a long way towards countering any nerves you may have and will help you respond in a clear, professional way.

Be unique

There is one important difference between interviews and exams: in an interview, you won't necessarily get through just because you know most or all of the answers. Your answers also have to be better than everyone else's. That's why learning sample answers from a book won't serve you as well as writing your own statements and answers. Sample answers may help you feel better on the day, but they can also make you sound clichéd and they certainly won't help you stand out.

It's a mistake many first-time interviewees make, learning stock answers online or from books. Possibly it's because up until the time you do your first job interview, most of the academic tests you have taken will be the kind that have right and wrong answers, and naturally you want to get yours right. But it really doesn't work that way.

No matter how much interview experience you have, the best way to rise above other candidates is for your answers to be well thought out and unique to you.

Answer preparation

There are two ways to tackle answer preparation: specifically and generally. Hopefully you have already prepared your first two statements – one about yourself, and one about why you want this job. This section goes into more detail on both, and considers the most common questions you are likely to be asked. No approach can prepare you for absolutely every question you will face, but we will look at the most common areas interviewers explore, and touch on techniques for handling tougher questions.

SPECIFIC APPROACH

The specific approach to answer preparation is recommended, whatever your level of interview experience. It takes a series of common interview questions and leads you through aspects you should consider when deciding how to answer each, including common mistakes and consistency. It also looks at different ways that the same question may be phrased.

The specific approach is great for first-timers as well as for helping more experienced job hunters prepare for a particular interview. It's an effective aid for learning to handle more challenging questions, including how to respond to a negatively phrased question with a positive answer. Examples and tips will help you devise your own statements and answers, and refine them until they show you in the best possible light. These notes will be your rehearsal aid before the interview, and once complete will help you prepare much faster for subsequent interviews.

Specific preparation
Step 1: Look at each question in the following chapters in turn.

Step 2: Prioritize the order in which you will prepare your answers according to the amount of time you have available before your interview.

Step 3: Create a Q&A crib sheet on which to keep all your notes. You can do this by hand but it's better done on screen to aid editing.

Step 4: Using the answer guides, write (or refine if you already have a crib sheet) your own answers and statements until you are happy they are relevant to this opportunity. Cut them until they are all under one minute.

Step 5: Practise your answers out loud, in front of a mirror. Change or simplify your wording if you keep stumbling over certain words or expressions.

GENERAL APPROACH

When done properly, the general approach is not necessarily quicker or easier; but, depending on your working style, you may prefer it.

Instead of focusing on the possible questions you could be asked and preparing answers to those, this approach creates an umbrella of 'preparedness' by encouraging you to think through your entire CV and career to date, teasing out all the skills you've learned and the decisions you've made along the way.

It works by getting you to think thoroughly about each part of your life (mainly your working life) and how this has equipped you and prepared you for the job you're now applying for. If you're the kind of person who is not particularly fazed by interviews, enjoys thinking on their feet and doesn't mind doing this in front of an interviewer, then this approach to preparation may suit you better.

General preparation

Step 1: For each section of the CV you applied with, explain how and why you decided upon each step you took within it. Why did you choose that course, that job, this company, that project, this team, that solution? Include why you didn't choose the alternatives. Using hindsight, note how good your decision was, what you learned (including specific skills) from the job or activity, and how you've applied that learning to benefit your work since.

Step 2: Go through your CV again, with the job advert/description next to you. If you're applying speculatively, use your estimated job advert based on your research.

Step 3: List all the skills, qualities and types of experience on your CV and the job description. For each, find two or three examples (recent ones are better) to show how you have applied this skill, quality or experience to the benefit of your employer. If there are any criteria in the job advert that you don't meet, think of any alternative skills you can offer in their place, along with supporting examples.

Insight

Support all claims with proof. In this context, a well-thought-out answer means a well-supported answer. Never make an empty claim: anyone can do that, so it gives you no advantage. Besides, you'll probably get caught out (now, or later) if your claims are groundless. By always giving examples, anecdotes or other proof to support what you are saying, you make yourself credible, unique and memorable.

Creating specific answers

Plan your answers, write notes, then refine them into something you can rehearse.

PLANNING AND WRITING ANSWERS

▶ Understand what the interviewer means by the question.
▶ Work out what information they're hoping to hear.
▶ Decide how many points you will make, and note down what to say for each.
▶ Be aware of danger areas (what *not* to say) and how to handle silence.
▶ Think about how to prove what you say is true and prepare two to three examples for each thing.

Insight

Give your answers the 'media treatment'. Never miss a trick to bring the subject around to a point you want to make, even if it wasn't strictly what you were asked about. Some politicians and company spokesmen do this very effectively, including positive 'sound bites' in all their answers, no matter how negatively framed or distantly related the question. You need to do this subtly, though – question dodgers are irritating.

REFINING ANSWERS

▶ Once you've constructed your basic answer following the above points, build in key words and phrases from the job advert or company website. Reflect their own language back to them.

- If necessary, cut your finished answer so it lasts no longer than one minute, including proof. If the interviewer is intrigued and wants more detail, they will ask. When in doubt about what to cut, be ruthless: stick to the most relevant and recent items.
- Keep anything you cut from an answer, such as additional examples of when you've used your skills, in your crib sheet notes – you may get asked follow-up questions that require further proof.

Insight

Once you've built some interview experience and feel comfortable with your answers, you can start refining answers on the spot. Choose words and phrases that reflect the interviewer's choice of language, especially jargon. You can also reflect the interviewer's tone: if they are excitable and animated, try to speak a similar way yourself, without parody. Reflecting your interviewer's style helps to build rapport. This is more confusing in panel interviews, as you have to reflect different styles, but it can be effective in securing everyone's vote.

FOCAL POINTS

- You'll feel more confident if you've prepared answers in advance.

- Stock answers don't offer a competitive edge; personal, unique answers do.

- Don't make the interviewer work hard: be clear, concise and relevant.

- Give answers the media treatment: talk about what YOU want to talk about.

- Reflect your interviewer's language and tone for maximum effect.

The 15 most common questions

In this chapter you will learn about:
- *the 15 most commonly asked questions and variations of them*
- *what they are really asking and trying to find out*
- *how you should, and – crucially – should not, respond to them.*

Question 1: Tell me about yourself.

If there is ever a question you should be ready to answer, it's this one. Your statement should be prepared, rehearsed and ready to deliver – although when you give your answer it still needs to sound natural and spontaneous. This question may also appear in slightly different guises:

▶ 'What should I know about you?'
▶ 'So, how did you come to be sitting here today?'

WHY IS IT BEING ASKED?

The interviewer wants a potted summary of why you think you're perfect for the job. They are NOT interested in your entire life history, only the relevant parts. Don't be fooled into thinking this is a general interest, chit-chat kind of question to break the ice and find out about you, the person behind the professional. It's not, even if it is the first thing out of the interviewer's mouth, and if you treat it like that, you'll be wasting a great opportunity to sell yourself.

COMMON MISTAKES

Treating the interviewer as a friend. If you start with: 'Well, I'm originally from Lancashire but moved to Scotland when I was a teenager. After I finished college in Edinburgh my family moved to

Hereford. I went with them and I've worked in this area ever since, firstly as an admin assistant and then as an accountant. Outside of work I'm a keen sailor and enjoy lots of sports...' what does this little spiel tell the interviewer about how well suited you are to their role? Or about how much you want to work for them? Very little. A friend might be interested in your life story, an interviewer is not.

WHAT TO INCLUDE

A *brief* summary of *relevant* points from your career history. Start with a little detail about your education, if it's both relevant and recent; otherwise mention the level to which you studied and move swiftly on to your work history.

Try to describe your career path very briefly but with key selling points. That means mentioning the company and the role, highlighting the value you brought to the company, the skills you used and any key achievements.

Insight

If you can, mention briefly what drew you to your next job (rather than focusing on what wasn't right in your previous role). This leads you neatly from job to job.

KEEP TO THE POINT

If you have more than three jobs to mention, stick to those relevant to the job you're being interviewed for. If they are all relevant, cluster similar roles together and mention them all in the same section.

For example, you could say that you gained this experience/performed brilliantly/developed those skills at Brag Ltd, Bluster plc and Swagger Associates, over a period of five years before joining Immodesty Inc.; and then go into a bit more detail about your key achievements and how you have added value to Immodesty Inc.

Example of a short career history

'At college I did a business administration course and started work as an admin assistant at the UK head office of Graduates Unlimited. Although I enjoyed the breadth of work, I wanted more of a challenge so I requested a secondment in accounting. I loved it.

'So for my next move, I chose a firm that would give me more demanding work and support me in gaining my CIMA qualifications. Five years ago I joined Willing & Abel, a small local accountancy firm, and by studying in my own time I passed the CIMA modules within two years. The fees I've since generated for the firm have far exceeded their investment in me, so I feel now is a good time to move on.

'My broad client experience and skills should be very valuable in a larger, more corporate environment such as yours; I'm good at seeing the bigger picture, I can turn my hand to almost anything and I'm keen to build more specialist client experience.

'I think Long, Term & Loyal Associates would be a great fit as I know you're looking for talented, recently qualified accountants like me, and that you strongly support continued professional development.'

Example of a longer career history

'From Cambridge University I went straight into medical sales, so I could use my biology degree and communication and interpersonal skills. I really wanted my contribution to be measurable, and there's nothing like a sales role for that. Over seven years I worked for five very different medical companies, from start-ups to blue-chip, and was consistently among the top three salespeople.

'The rewards were excellent but the medical field rather limited, so I moved to a senior sales job in the rapidly growing telecoms industry. I quickly gained relevant experience and targeted a regional sales management role.

'In the decade since then I've successfully run large sales teams of up to 60 people, for global companies based in Australia, the UK and the US. I've become an excellent motivator with a relaxed, informal management style and I'm also personally responsible for MaxCom's success with new business development, so I'm very much leading by example.

'With the breadth of industry, management and geographical experience I've gained, and my strategic approach to new business, I feel I'm now ready for the role of sales director.'

LENGTH

This last example is about the same length as the first, with four main points, yet it spans a much longer career. By sticking to the highlights, clustering roles and not mentioning every company name – the key ones will be in your CV anyway – you can keep your answer to a reasonable length. If you're still struggling, remove any duplications and then start deleting the least relevant parts of your history (perhaps the oldest).

LOGIC

What's important for this type of statement or answer is being able to draw some sort of thread through your career. You need to try and make it sound as if your career path to this point makes sense, and was somehow planned to turn out this way, rather than being down to pure fate and coincidence (even if it was).

Question 2: What attracts you to this job/company?

This may also appear as:

- ▶ 'Which other jobs/companies have you applied for?'
- ▶ 'Why here, why not company X?'
- ▶ 'In your opinion, what would be the best and worst parts about working here?'
- ▶ 'What's important to you in a job/employer?'

WHY IS IT BEING ASKED?

Quite simply they want to know if you want *this* opportunity, or just *any* opportunity. If you join without consideration, you're more likely to leave without consideration – and probably sooner rather than later. The interviewer wants to know you've thought through your reasons for applying for this job, with this company, at this time.

COMMON MISTAKES

However the question may sound, merely saying what you'd selfishly like to get out of this job or company is not what they want to hear. Your answer should still be pitched in terms of what your skills are and why you want to bring them to this role and company.

Nor do you have to spill the beans about exactly where else you may have applied. If you start off with a list of ten other companies you're applying to, you could end up getting a bit sidetracked. Always start with what you were looking for, and therefore what drew you to this opportunity, so the focus stays on you and on the skills you could bring.

Finally, if asked what appeals most and least about an opportunity, don't ever say: 'Well, if I'm honest, I'm really not looking forward to X.' Remain focused on the positives; if pushed for something negative, you can always say you haven't found anything that's put you off yet.

WHAT TO INCLUDE

Demonstrate that you have done your research, that you know what the company and its products and services are like, and why your skill set and personality would be a great addition. Be sure to pick out the most appealing aspects of the company; perhaps its position in the marketplace or reputation for investing in staff development.

The same applies to the role you are after. Show that you have taken time to understand what the job actually involves. Talk about how your abilities, knowledge and experience make you likely to be very successful in doing it and why you'd enjoy this challenge.

KEEP TO THE POINT

Don't let yourself get distracted by other opportunities you're pursuing – stick to what you know about this company and this role, and why this is the one for you. You only have one minute.

EXAMPLE

Example – why this role?

'So, why do you want to work in customer service / this role?'

'Because I believe that a company's relationship with its customers is at the heart of its success, and I want to be a part of that success.

'I really enjoy being able to see and hear the impact of my work, so a role like this where results depend on my interpersonal skills, knowledge and quick thinking would be really satisfying.

'In the longer term there is plenty of opportunity to progress within customer service, and to influence customers from a more senior perspective, so as a career it offers everything I'm looking for.'

Example – what's important?

'*What's important to you in a job?*'
'I'm after a job where I can make a contribution right from the start, and with my strong interpersonal skills I think I can do that here.

'How a company relates to its customers, especially under difficult circumstances, is really important. The research I've done suggests that this is very much a priority for you, and your reputation for customer service is really good, so that's why I'm particularly keen on this job opportunity.'

Example – why here?

'*Which other companies have you applied to?*'

'*Why here, why not company X?*'

'*What would be the best and worst parts about working here?*'

'Well, I've focused on companies that view customer service as a priority. The research I've done online and within the industry has highlighted that it is a particular priority for JEP, and your reputation for customer service is strong, so that's why I'm keen on this opportunity.

'I like working in a role that directly contributes to company performance – I like a challenge, I enjoy pressure and I believe it would make great use of the excellent telephone skills I've developed from working on the Samaritans helpline.'

When answering the first two questions you could include:

'I'd consider applying to other companies with similar values and reputations, in any industry – although I'm particularly keen on retail.'

For the final question, you could add:

'I haven't yet come across any negative aspects of working here during my research, but if there's anything you think I should know, please say!'

LENGTH

Don't waffle: stick to what you've found out about the role/company and why it resonates with you. There's nothing wrong with a short answer.

Insight

If you've gone above and beyond with your research, looking out previous employees, suppliers and agencies that have worked for or with the company, you may wish to briefly mention how you've gone about getting this information: it helps prove you're serious about this job.

LOGIC

There should be an overall consistency to your answer: what you've researched about the company or role should match why your skills make you a suitable candidate and what appeals to you most about the opportunity.

If you cannot justify another job you've applied for, keep quiet about it. You can say you're in the early stages of job hunting and still doing your research. Focus only on the sort of role or employer you're looking for and why this one fits the bill.

If you do admit to applying for another role, and the interviewer spots an inconsistency in your logic, you can either admit the mistake and say you'll be asking about that at interview, or acknowledge that on paper the opportunity doesn't look as good as this one, but you like to evaluate all options.

Better still, don't allow yourself to get drawn into discussing your other applications in the first place. The only exception is if you apply for jobs at two companies owned by the same parent company; they might not compare notes, but you'd be as well to mention it anyway.

Question 3: How well do you match this job vacancy?

Avoid panicking if this question comes hot on the heels of Question 2: you may need to repeat yourself a little, but there's nothing like repetition to help an interviewer remember your best points. You may also hear the following:

▶ 'Why do you think this is the job for you?'
▶ 'Tell me, why would you be good at this job?'
▶ 'What would make you better at this job than other candidates?'
▶ 'So, do you have what we're looking for?'

WHY IS IT BEING ASKED?

The interviewer is asking you to make it easy for them. In one minute, explain just how close you come to being their perfect candidate. A second and probably lesser reason is that they may wish to test whether you know (and remember) the criteria listed in the job advert.

COMMON MISTAKES

Don't be fooled into thinking that this question needs a full and frank admission of just how closely you do or don't meet the various job criteria. Why raise a negative yourself? That's not to say you shouldn't think about how to answer if the interviewer does note any gaps in your skill set or experience and questions you about them in detail; but it's certainly not something you should intentionally bring to their attention.

WHAT TO INCLUDE

Talk about how good a match you are; skip anything that doesn't support your case. You should have been through all the criteria in the job advert in detail when writing your tailored CV. Ideally you will have focused on how well you match these criteria in your summary statement or profile at the top of your CV. Take those four or five points and expand on each one briefly by mentioning an example that supports what you are claiming.

KEEP TO THE POINT

Leave out any of your strengths that aren't mentioned in the job advert. This is not asking about your general brilliance but about how well you meet their criteria.

An exception would be if you possess something not mentioned in the job advert that you believe would be a real advantage – if you would bring with you an existing network of useful contacts, for example. If so, you can add this to the end of your answer and explain briefly why you feel it's relevant.

Example

'I have five years' part-time retail experience with Superior Supermarkets. I've proven my motivation and commitment by holding that job down throughout my A level and university studies.

'I've also shown I'm good at working with others, analysing information and coming up with recommendations. For example, I noticed that staff handled stock and deliveries differently in each of the four Superior branches I've worked at. So I emailed head office to suggest that a central stock management process be defined and rolled out, with a full-time employee at each branch responsible for implementing it. I was invited to be part of the project team and it was a great success: sell-through improved, less space was taken up with unsold stock, and there was less wastage overall.

'In summary, I believe I have the full range of experience and abilities you're looking for, as well as being a proven team player with loads of commitment and motivation.'

LENGTH

There may be lots more you could say, and examples (proof) you could mention – but this should start as a one-minute answer.

Restrict any examples you give to the highest priorities listed in the job advert.

However, also prepare one or two further examples of each skill or characteristic that you can use if the interviewer asks for more evidence of any of them.

LOGIC

It's straightforward: select the job criteria you meet in order of importance, and give the interviewer some proof. Don't bring up any criteria that you don't meet, but be ready with a positive story if the interviewer asks about those separately.

Question 4: What do you know about the job/company/products?

Could also be phrased as:

▶ 'What research did you do in preparation for this interview?'

WHY IS IT BEING ASKED?

This is a direct question to see whether you did your homework on the company and the role before applying or coming for interview. The fact that it's one of the most commonly asked questions is proof in itself that interviewers value candidates who do their research.

The research you do should inform or shape most of your prepared answers anyway, but this question will instantly show how much effort you have put into it. In theory, the keener you are to win this job (measured by the amount of research you did), the more motivated you'll be to do whatever it takes to succeed if you get it.

COMMON MISTAKES

The worst thing you can do is pay lip service to research – it really is the barometer for any interviewer to gauge how serious you are about the job. You might be pleasantly surprised by just how much research can count for at interview. Being able to do the job is important, but doing your research can help you to leapfrog past people who, on paper, are more qualified than you.

Another error is to do the research but not learn it. You'll never convince an interviewer you spent hours online and calling contacts if you can't remember what you found out. Try to learn as much as possible by heart; if you don't think you'll be able to remember all the key points, you can always make some brief notes to take into the interview with you.

WHAT TO INCLUDE

Mention your research sources – that way even if some of the elements aren't strictly correct, you've shown yourself resourceful enough to use all available routes to getting that information. Include the Internet, visiting libraries, checking newspaper archives, inspecting or buying products, calling their customer service department, using all your personal contacts.

You can also mention how much time you've spent on research; this goes some way towards showing your genuine desire for the job. You may have amassed quite a lot of information, so the key here will be prioritizing what to talk about and leaving out chunks that aren't really important.

Insight

It can be worth including one fact that is particularly unusual or which really interested you; ideally something that other candidates wouldn't mention. If you can leave the interviewer thinking 'Wow, they're the only person who knew we just won a major award/five-year contract/government funding,' then you'll have gained the edge.

KEEP TO THE POINT

As with many interview answers, if you can summarize the information clearly and concisely it says great things about your communication skills. Rather than rattling off a series of facts about the company and/or job, restrict yourself to five or six of the most relevant details. Relevant means anything related to you, your strengths and your future career. As you mention each point or area you discovered, explain why it appealed to you or why it would make you a good fit with the organization.

'I spent around six hours on research, starting with your website.

'I like that you're still family-owned, despite being such a large company with subsidiaries across Europe – you should be more flexible, react faster to change and be able to take more risks. That appeals to me more than working for a shareholder-oriented company.

'Your annual reports show you've grown over the past two years, mainly due to your latest product launches. I'm familiar with many of your products as a customer as well as a designer; my favourite is the Spada range and the way each product shares the family look while being so individual.

'I also learned that, although your head office is in Manchester, the R&D facility is based here in Reading: that's ideal for me, although I can relocate if needed.

'Finally, I checked the latest trade press releases and saw you have another new range launching before Christmas, which suggests your R&D department will be dynamic as well as innovative. That's exactly the kind of environment I thrive in, as a designer of fresh and eye-catching brands.'

LENGTH

Keep to one minute. Anything else you think you want to add, don't – not at this point. If the interviewer asks you what else you found out, or what you found most interesting or surprising, then you can add further comments – but make sure you keep relating them to you.

LOGIC

The logic behind your answer needs to be twofold. First try to start with any overview information (company structure, business, locations, ethos) before drilling down into details that you particularly relate to.

Secondly, ensure that each piece of information you mention allows you to reveal something of your own skills or how it makes you more eager to get the job. Suggesting that the more you found out about the company and the job, the more enthusiastic you became, will count in your favour.

Question 5: Why do/did you want to leave your current/last job?

Maybe it's laziness, maybe it's because deep down most people don't enjoy change, but it's human nature to look for a new job only once we start to feel negative about our current job. Far fewer people leave while they're on a high because they've spotted the perfect next move for them.

This query may also manifest itself as:

- ▶ 'Why don't you like working where you do just now?'
- ▶ 'How come you're unemployed at the moment?'
- ▶ 'What made you leave company X; surely there was plenty of scope for development?'

WHY IS IT BEING ASKED?

It's natural to want to know what made someone ditch their previous jobs. Perhaps there is a pattern. The interviewer may feel that knowing the reasons behind your past career moves will predict whether you'll stick around this time, or whether there's something that will lead you to the door sooner than they'd like.

It's also often asked as an intentionally negative question; it's far less common to be asked what attracted you to a particular job, which would encourage you to bring out the positives.

COMMON MISTAKES

Try not to directly address your reasons for leaving unless they are positive, such as development and promotion, or beyond your control like redundancy or relocation. If you privately detest your boss, keep that as your little secret. Avoid mentioning any problems with management, flings with colleagues or company financial troubles; in fact, don't focus on anything negative.

If you leave behind a trail which includes a forced resignation, dismissal for gross misconduct, ill-considered career moves, an employment tribunal or any other legal battle, try and steer clear of these. Any issues with a previous employer can taint your chances of being taken on, even if you were ultimately blameless and behaved impeccably.

WHAT TO INCLUDE

You need to come across as a positive, loyal, dependable and committed employee – not a dissatisfied whiner who will jump ship at the first sign of any trouble. That means only talking about the positives: bring up what drew you to each new opportunity, rather than whatever made you leave the previous one behind. Don't be scared to disagree with the way the question is phrased.

Aim to do this in a way that gives the impression you did (and still do) have some sort of a career plan.

KEEP TO THE POINT

As usual, anything that allows you to talk through your work history should be used as a chance to highlight your relevant selling points – how well you performed, which skills you want to use more, and which you'd like to develop further.

Redundancy should be treated in exactly the same way: it can happen to anyone and is unrelated to job performance, and you still need to put everything positively. By all means touch on the circumstances of your redundancy very briefly and objectively, but spend most of your time talking about the good things that came from it – training perhaps, or new skills, new opportunities, a better role, a change of career path, or whatever it was.

Example of a clear career path

'My current role is great, actually. I've really taken to working in logistics over the past 18 months. I've enjoyed getting everyone working as a team, to reduce operating costs and improve delivery timings and accuracy. And now I'm ready for my next challenge.

'With every move I've looked to expand my retail experience, with the aim of becoming a store manager. I've worked in every area from supply chain to sales, marketing and even training. I've built up detailed operational understanding and proved my ability to motivate different teams.

'I feel it's the right time for me to go for a store manager role, and this looked perfect. I feel ready to deliver against store targets and develop more formal management skills.'

Example of a 'dotted-about career'

'Actually I can't say there's anything I dislike about my current job – my boss and my colleagues are all brilliant to work with. The team is really motivated and professional and the working atmosphere is great; leaving them will probably be the hardest part. But throughout my career I've always looked to gain and apply new skills.

'At Wolf Doors Ltd I developed my communication; Hand to Mouth taught me about building relationships and teams. Dreaming Spires brought out my creative thinking; Sensory Foods was focused on process efficiency. Now I'm looking for a project management role that will benefit from all these proven skills, and in a larger company where I can develop professionally over the longer term.'

Example for 'How come you're unemployed just now?'

'Our department was made redundant with less than a week's notice, and I've been keen to finish the step I'd started to make in my last job. I was making the move from programming to new business development. I have a great mix of interpersonal skills and technical understanding, and I can communicate complex problems and solutions easily to clients. Since the department closed I've been busy adding to my skills, with training courses on advanced presentations and project management. I now feel totally ready for the challenges of new business development, and I believe this is the right role.'

LENGTH

Keep your answer as short as possible. Don't feel you need to use the whole minute.

The logic needs to come from having a career plan. If your career has darted about all over the place because you switched to whatever was immediately available whenever you fell out with a manager or wanted a pay rise, you may need to spend much more time thinking of a plausible rationale than if you've followed a clearer career path.

Question 6: What are your strengths?

This can also be phrased more specifically, by asking you the question from any number of different perspectives:

'What are your strengths...

- ▶ ...in your opinion?'
- ▶ ...as others see them?'
- ▶ ...from your current boss's viewpoint?'
- ▶ ...according to your co-workers?'
- ▶ ...would your friends say?'
- ▶ ...in the eyes of your enemies?'

This question could also be asked in many other ways, including:

- ▶ 'What qualities do you have that you feel work well with other people?'
- ▶ 'In what ways are you a good technician/communicator/ salesman/counsellor/social worker?'

WHY IS IT BEING ASKED?

- ▶ The 'strengths' question might seem a bit of a cliché, but the reason it's still in the top 15 is because it never fails to highlight *something* interesting about a candidate. Whether it's your own strengths you actually manage to highlight, someone else's, or something else entirely, is down to how you answer.

COMMON MISTAKES

Not thinking about what you have to offer in advance is a common mistake. If this question takes you by surprise, you'll miss an opportunity to sell yourself. It could also make you seem unaware of your abilities or give the impression you don't notice feedback from others.

WHAT TO INCLUDE

Everyone has strengths: it's just a case of finding the best way to describe these in a work context. Depending on how specific the question is – i.e. whether it's your opinion they want, or that of others – you can answer in different ways.

If it's your own opinion you are venturing, also offer solid examples to support your claim to have a particular strength. If it's the opinion of others, it can be quite powerful to use testimonials from your boss, from an appraisal, in memos or emails; even hearsay is worth mentioning, as long as it's true. Anything someone else (who you can identify with a name and job title) has said about you adds credibility to your statements. In fact, even if you're not asked about other perspectives, a testimonial can still be a very powerful addition to your answer.

KEEP TO THE POINT

For each perspective prepare not just one, but *three* strengths that you can talk about comfortably and provide supporting evidence for. Try to pick three that relate to the job criteria so that you are reinforcing your application rather than randomly identifying strengths. If you can't relate them to the job, pick your best and most transferable strengths rather than niche abilities.

Examples

The job advert calls for an experienced project manager who is excellent at building relationships, is a decisive leader, can be an inspiration to the whole team and has the confidence to deliver multimillion dollar projects within tight constraints.

'What would your team say your main strength is?'

'I ask for regular feedback from every team I lead, and the most frequent thing I hear is that I'm a very motivational person. A recent project I managed, launching a prototype data storage system, met with technical setback after setback because the technology was so new. I remained consistently supportive to all involved but above all I was always honest with them about our progress, because I knew that being well informed was motivational for them. The whole team worked their socks off for me and managed to meet the final deadline against the odds.'

'What else might they mention?'

'They've also said I'm happy to give all team members a chance to contribute to discussions, that I'm not afraid to make decisions and take responsibility for them. I run weekly project meetings as these are a very useful forum for brainstorming issues, identifying risks, and deciding on strategy. I'm also quite protective if problems arise; I handle them myself and always protect my team from fallout.'

LENGTH

Keep it brief by describing just one strength at a time, in order of importance, with proof of how it's benefited your employers. Up to one minute is fine.

The interviewer may well ask you for a second, and a third, each of which again could be up to a minute long. If they ask for more than three, think on your feet and refer back to your summary statement for anything else relevant to the job that you could mention.

LOGIC

Put across your strengths in a *balanced* way: you can have too much of a good thing. Attention to detail is useful in many jobs but someone who can't see past that detail is a liability. A great sense of humour might develop into an inability to take anything seriously. Be aware of both sides.

....
Insight
Talking about your strengths is the best chance to promote yourself and be memorable, so a smart answer can be worth the risk, provided it rings true:

Q: *'What is your greatest strength? Can you tell me about a recent time when you used it to good effect?'*

A: *'Brevity. Just now.'*

► Your answer and its supporting evidence are all provided in three words. It has to be sincere though: this wouldn't wash if you're a natural waffler.

Question 7: What are your weaknesses?

Like the strengths question just before, this can be made much more specific by asking the question from different perspectives.

WHY IS IT BEING ASKED?

Interviewers like employees who are self-aware, particularly when it comes to weaknesses. They believe that employees who are aware of their weaker aspects are able to appraise their own performance effectively, and will be likely to want to improve their skills. This sort of employee, the kind who is constantly learning and developing, will become more valuable to an organization over time.

This isn't a universal truth: some people know their own faults but are very defensive about them, or want people to accept them just as they are. So when you answer, make it clear that you are an improver and not a coaster.

COMMON MISTAKES

Having a weakness that is listed as a critical requirement in the job advert. Mentioning testimonials: don't add credibility to any negative points by saying that others have noticed them too! If you do have to say what your weaknesses are from another person's perspective, then try to answer as if you were thinking of what they *might* say, rather than what they *have* said. Trying to turn a negative into a positive is reasonable, accepted and even expected in an interview. But don't fall for the myth that you should state a weakness that can also be perceived as a strength. Internet chat rooms abound with people promoting the idea that your 'weakness' should be something like:

- ► working too hard
- ► being a perfectionist
- ► too enthusiastic/passionate

- ▶ too much attention to detail
- ▶ being too ambitious/competitive
- ▶ an inability to lie.

Interviewers, especially experienced ones, are a fairly cynical bunch. Many will feel virtually obliged to ignore your answer if you bring up any of the above or something similar. This might not lose you the job, but it doesn't say anything particularly positive about you or your originality.

Insight

Cynicism aside, each of the above 'weaknesses that are strengths' could also be a serious fault when taken to extremes. Burnt-out workaholics cannot give their best, nor can perfectionists who never complete a task, obsessives who are blind to risk, a detail person who lacks strategic focus, or the ambitious executive who climbs over others. People who 'can't lie' probably do, or are so brutally honest that no one ever seeks their opinion.

Other people feel that the best option is to mention a weakness that doesn't really impact on their ability to do their job. This could be just about anything:

- ▶ 'I'm a bit vain about my appearance.'
- ▶ 'I can never say no to my mother.'
- ▶ 'I'm a rubbish cook/gardener/storyteller/actor/hairdresser.'
- ▶ 'I'm a bit of a softie – I'd give someone my purse if they had a good sob story.'
- ▶ 'I'm terrible in bed.'

Yes, it may not affect your ability to do the job but the interviewer may wonder why on earth you're bringing up something so personal, inappropriate or irrelevant in a job interview. Or their reply might be 'I meant in a work context', which neatly squashes any attempt to avoid their question.

WHAT TO INCLUDE

Instead of mentioning 'a weakness that can also be a strength' and leaving it to the interviewer to interpret, find a genuine weakness of yours. But make sure it's a weakness that has a limited impact on your work – because you are aware of it and therefore do your best to consciously minimize it.

Any weakness that used to cause you problems but that you have largely conquered in a work context – through practice, mentoring, education, training or even counselling – would be an appropriate answer. In some cases you may even have turned your weakness to your advantage.

Even if you only answer with one weakness to start with, interviewers are aware that most people do the bare minimum of preparation so they'll likely ask you for another weakness just to throw you off balance and see what else you come up with. So my advice is to prepare at least three weaknesses and evidence of how you've improved upon them over time.

KEEP TO THE POINT

The point you want to make is that your weakness has a limited impact on your work (and employer), so avoid getting sidetracked about how much trouble this caused you or them in the past, and instead focus on the positive evidence that you are seeing improvements in this area. Finish on a positive.

Example

EXAMPLE

'Some feedback from a customer in my first sales job really struck home. They bought from me, but jokingly said if I'd talked half as much, they might have bought double. My manager acknowledged that I was a good listener but did tend to talk too much when enthusiastic, so I asked if I could go on an advanced communication skills course. This used video playback of role-play sessions, which made me very aware of how I was coming across, and I worked hard to address it. I still consciously control my communication but it's starting to become second nature; I believe it's getting this balance right that helped me top the sales league this year.'

LENGTH

Up to one minute, but let's face it – you're talking about weaknesses, so the less time spent on it the better; unless you have a really great anecdote about how you're turning it all around.

Be consistent: you may be turning something that is a weakness into a positive trait, but you can't use the same characteristic as one of your main strengths when asked. Keep your answers to these two questions totally separate.

Question 8: What's been your biggest success/challenge/disappointment/mistake/failure/decision/regret to date?

WHY IS IT BEING ASKED?

To get into the sort of goals you set yourself; whether you've had any important successes and how you measure them; how you have learned from your mistakes, and how you handle failure or disappointment.

COMMON MISTAKES

Dwelling on negatives. The longer you spend on these, however honest you'd like to be, the more the interviewer will associate negative traits with you. Negative aspects should be skimmed over so the main focus is optimistic and ends on a positive note: how you worked through something to become a more efficient and valuable employee.

At the other extreme, 'I can't recall ever having made a mistake at work, actually.' This is a bit like being the driver who says 'I keep seeing terrible accidents in my rear-view mirror, thank goodness I've never been involved in one,' but has no idea that they're causing the crashes when others try to compensate for their terrible driving. It's unlikely you've never made a mistake, so the cynical questioner could assume you are:

- ▶ inexcusably arrogant
- ▶ lying through your teeth
- ▶ totally unaware of your mistakes (a real liability)
- ▶ still looking for your first job.

WHAT TO INCLUDE

The question looks like just so many ways of asking the same thing, but it isn't. Choose carefully what to talk about in each case.

Success

This could be anything you choose, but if you can make it work-related (ideally, relevant to *this* job) then so much the better.

Whether a work or a personal success, make sure it shows some of the essential skills they are looking for. Perhaps you raised funds for a cause you were passionate about, and exceeded your target. Make sure to mention the people or businesses you *communicated* with, *presented* to and *persuaded*, or perhaps the team of volunteers you *managed*, how you *set targets* or *monitored progress*.

Also mention why this is the stand-out success you've chosen to talk about: perhaps it was the tangible impact on real people that did it for you.

Example

'I think it would be when I set out to raise £1,000 for Redun Dance, a charity providing dance lessons to the unemployed, and managed to raise over ten times that.

'I myself benefited from the charity when I was made redundant three years ago – it's surprising how much physical movement can energize you while you're head down applying for jobs. Once I was working again I wanted to give something back.

'I wanted to raise the charity's profile as well as funds, so I went for corporate sponsorship on one side, presenting to a number of carefully chosen companies to persuade them to support the programme in the longer term. On the other side, I co-ordinated a network of volunteers to set up an annual fundraising event. The very first event raised over £3,000, while corporate sponsorship of £7,500 brought us in over the £10k mark.

'Having heard from some of the people who benefited from these funds, I can honestly say this is my greatest success to date.'

Challenge

You can interpret this as 'the bit leading up to your greatest success'. It's always better to talk about a challenge you overcame than one that got the better of you.

If you take the above example as your 'success':

'Well, it was when I was raising funds for Redun Dance. The biggest challenge was to take a disparate group of local volunteers, who each had different skills, motivations and ideas about how they wanted to work, and putting them together into a co-ordinated fundraising team.

'It took all my interpersonal skills to encourage, influence, flatter and persuade these volunteers to work together and support each other in one common aim. I found that regular updates and group meetings made the biggest difference, so that they all got to know each other better and could see the tangible benefits of working together rather than on individual initiatives.

'But the hard work paid off and last summer we successfully ran our first major fundraising event – a sponsored dance-off and fete in the local park. It raised over £3,000, three times what we'd expected, and the team were really proud of what they achieved. Plans are underway to make it an annual event.'

Disappointment

This should be something you didn't manage first time, but didn't give up on and later succeeded at in some way. The disappointment can be as monumental as you like, provided the follow-up and turnaround is positive. Your answer needs to show you took action to turn disappointment into satisfaction, and you may find a personal example illustrates this just as well as an example from work.

'Up until I was 19 I was on track to become a professional footballer, when – as is so often the case – a bad knee injury ruined my chances. I was more disappointed than you can imagine, but focused instead on getting back to full fitness.

'It took four hours of physiotherapy and training every day for over a year, and during that time I came to terms with the fact I would not be able to play for a living. But football was still my passion, so I changed direction and began to coach the under 13s at my local club.

'I've found it takes a lot of communication, persuasion and leadership to inspire kids to play at their best – and that coaching is far more satisfying than focusing on your own abilities.'

Mistake

This isn't a 'who cocked up most this year' competition. The kind of tales you spin at the pub about your misdeeds might be entertaining, but you need a different approach to share a mistake with an interviewer.

Like some of the other categories within this question, this answer is all about what *you* learned from your mistake, and how your performance has changed for the better ever since. Mistakes you learn from show that you are aware where you went wrong, and took steps to fix it to avoid any repeats.

If you haven't worked before, even in a holiday job, try to think of a time you made a mistake at home, school or university. Then say what you changed as a result and how this new awareness/trait/skill could benefit this employer.

Example

'During my A levels I worked at the local veterinary laboratories, learning how to handle hazardous materials, plate out bacteria samples and perform complex virus tests.

'I was praised for the quality of my work for the first three days, but then made a mistake with a virus test. I marked the result positive, but my supervisor challenged it before the results went out. She explained that my mistake could have had consequences: a false positive would have resulted in a pet being put down unnecessarily.

'This really struck home and after that I took extra care with all the test procedures – even simple ones. The experience stayed with me; attention to detail is now one of my greatest assets.'

Failure

Failure can be taken to be the same as 'mistake', if failure is what resulted from your mistake. Or failure can mean very simply not achieving a target, whether you or someone else set it. Ideally show that you managed to achieve the target (or a similar goal) in a later attempt. This demonstrates perseverance.

Example

'About five years ago I wanted to be promoted to team leader. On paper I had all the skills required for the job, but found myself up against two candidates who had some management experience already.

'When I failed to get the promotion I asked the hiring manager what else I'd have needed to demonstrate to get the job, and based on his comments I made a few changes. Within my normal role I asked if I could take on additional responsibilities that included more management-oriented tasks, and I was sponsored for an internal leadership course.

'Eighteen months later, when the opportunity arose again, I was better prepared and got the promotion I'd wanted. That was despite being up against older candidates with more experience again.'

Regret

This could be similar to failure, although regret is a more difficult one as it smacks of something you wish had never happened (or something you wish you'd done, but didn't).

Having a regret could also imply that it's still eating at you; otherwise you'd have moved on or accepted it by now. So what you admit to regretting can suggest unresolved issues. It is perfectly possible that you don't have any regrets, especially in a work context. If that's the case, say so.

EXAMPLE

'For me, regret is something that applies to something you didn't do, or a chance you didn't take. I've always taken every opportunity that came my way, and worked as hard as possible to make each one a success, so I don't really have any regrets.'

LENGTH

For any of these questions, keep your answer to one minute – and make sure most of that time is spent on the positive aspects and what you did, rather than on anything that went wrong. You may be asked to elaborate on certain aspects but your initial response should still be brief.

LOGIC

There should be a thread running through all these answers – whatever circumstances throw at you, you can see what needs to be done, are able to take appropriate action, end up in a better place than where you started (be that mentally or physically), and learn from it to enhance your future performance.

Question 9: What have you learned this past year/decade/since leaving school/university/ your last job?

WHY IS IT BEING ASKED?

Two reasons. First, it's a good way for interviewers to see how you view your own progress or development over time. Secondly, most organizations spend a large part of their time communicating information. Candidates who show they can summarize large amounts of information in a clear, simple way are worth their weight in gold.

COMMON MISTAKES

Saying too much or too little: 'Well, I've not learned much really, it's only been a few months' or 'I've been around the block several times;

I don't think there's much I don't already know' would be classed as too little. Employers want people who constantly strive to do better and monitor their own progress; not someone who doesn't care, or who thinks they already know everything.

Not being able to summarize your learning succinctly is another common mistake. Don't feel you have to go into what you've learned in great detail, unless asked.

WHAT TO INCLUDE

If you can, focus on talking about any skills you've learned that are also required for this job. It gives you another chance to remind the interviewer that you have what they're looking for. It's often easier to do this if they're asking about a long time span. Try to touch briefly on the benefits your learning has brought to your employers, by way of proof.

Insight

If it's a short time span they're enquiring about, then make sure you find something, anything, which falls within that time frame. If you gained all your relevant skills long ago, talk about how you've polished or practised those existing skills recently, and some of the advantages this has brought.

Make your answer structured: try choosing three things you have learned and mention them all up front. Then place each one in a 12 to 15-second sentence which explains what you learned, when/how you learned it, and why it has been useful in your job.

KEEP TO THE POINT

Focus on the desirable skills you now possess, through training or practice, and how these have improved your performance at work and suitability for this role. Follow a logical structure if possible.

Don't just rattle off the names of courses you've attended, when and where. If the interviewer is interested in anything in particular, they can always ask follow-up questions.

Example

'What have you learned since starting your current job?'

'Better attention to detail, reporting and analytical skills. I applied for a position in market planning because, although I'm very numerate, I'd only worked in field sales and wanted to build experience on the supply and forecasting side.

'In my role I process a huge amount of information, which feeds into the manufacturing plan, so the impact of getting even one digit out of place can be huge; my attention to detail has improved vastly. I've learned to analyse data quickly and accurately, and I now use this to sense-check sales forecasts, challenging any figures that look unrealistic.

'Much of my time has been spent finding out what other departments – including finance, sales and the management team – really need to know about. Tailoring my regular reports more effectively has gained me some excellent feedback.

'Together, everything I've learned has helped to raise the profile of forecasting within the company. As a result we now have far less wastage, which means a previously unprofitable area is finally turning a profit.'

Example

'What have you learned in the last month?'

'Communication and presenting have always been strengths for me, and I've put them to good use in every role I've had; it's been key to my success in meeting all the different challenges of marketing new products.

'Then about three weeks ago, I did something I'd never tried before – a public speaking course – and I was surprised to find how quickly it raised my skills up another notch.

'When on my feet I now feel more comfortable than ever before, and I've begun two new initiatives supported by the sales director. I now deliver detailed product training sessions to the entire sales force – the first one last week received brilliant feedback – and support senior account managers with joint pitches to major clients.

'Working closer together like this has already helped us to win three new accounts.'

LENGTH

Follow the usual rules and keep it to one minute – the interviewer can always ask for more.

Question 10: Why should you be the person we hire for this job?

This classic may also be phrased as:

▶ 'What makes you better than the other candidates?'
▶ 'How will you impress me more than anyone else does?'

WHY IS IT BEING ASKED?

This question is just yet another way of asking you how well you meet the job criteria and what you can bring to the company – it's just phrased in a more competitive-sounding way.

COMMON MISTAKES

Don't take this question too literally; you really don't need to stalk other candidates to confirm whether you are better, or to dig up dirty little secrets to use against them. You may not even see any of the other candidates on interview day and, even if you did, casting them in a negative light to make yourself look good is NOT what this question is about.

WHAT TO INCLUDE

How you answer depends on how many questions you have already been asked like this, or whether this is one of the first questions of your interview.

If it's the opening question, or soon after:

▶ For each key requirement of the job, prove (by citing examples) how well you meet it. These examples should be SHORT-listed (ideally the ones in your CV, if good).

▶ Cover the most critical job criteria (with examples to back up your statements) first, so you don't run out of time, then briefly mention the rest without proof.

If you're quite some way into the interview, then try to avoid being too repetitive. For each key requirement of the role, very briefly summarize or acknowledge what you've already discussed. Add any relevant criteria that you haven't been asked about yet, and offer brief proof of these, too.

KEEP TO THE POINT

If you find yourself saying anything at all about other candidates, stop. You don't want to be talking about them or for the interviewer to be thinking about them at all; this is YOUR interview.

Example where this is an early question

'I can't speak for any of the other candidates, but I can say that I bring with me the ten years' varied retail experience you're asking for, yet my eyes are still fresh.

'Introducing and managing strategic change at every level is not new to me, as you'll see from my success in bringing Growing Green, Petal Power, Cheesy Deals and Fishy Fresh together into a single market co-operative.

'My process and analytical skills are well developed from having worked closely with IT consultancies to design stock control and logistics systems for hi-tech retailers, and these skills proved essential to improving supply chain efficiency for two major regional grocers.

'I believe I offer all the key elements you're looking for, and that my talents would be perfectly suited to modernizing your supply chain.'

Example where this is a later question

'Well, as we've discussed, my management style is very much the open, relaxed style you are looking for. The five years I spent in Human Resources means I'm well versed in employment issues and how to handle them, as in the examples I mentioned earlier.

'Managing a whole department through the kind of change facing your company right now can be really challenging. I believe my successes with Merger and Merger Ltd prove that I have the right mix of interpersonal, communication and leadership skills to deliver massive change and yet still keep the whole team's commitment and support.'

LENGTH

Keep your answer under one minute if this is an early question. If you don't have time to cover examples of some of your skills, name-drop them at the end of your answer anyway – the interviewer can always ask you to elaborate.

Make your answer half as long if you're summarizing topics already covered earlier in the interview. Do this by leaving out any examples or detail you've already discussed.

LOGIC

Follow the logic of the job advert – which criteria you need to mention and in which order – and the logic of the interview – which areas you've already discussed.

Question 11: How do you work as part of a team?

Also may be phrased as:

- ▶ 'What sort of a team player are you?'
- ▶ 'Are you a team player?'
- ▶ 'Do you prefer to work alone or with others?'
- ▶ 'How do you share out tasks when working as a group?'

WHY IS IT BEING ASKED?

This question can be interpreted as 'How well are you going to fit in with the people you'll be working with?' Without knowing them, and without them knowing you, this can be tough to answer, but the job advert might give you a useful guide. Make an educated guess as to what they're likely to be looking for, even if they don't state it directly in the job advert.

COMMON MISTAKES

Not bothering to find out what sort of person they are looking for. You could easily rule yourself out by not pitching yourself appropriately.

Being too prescriptive about your working style. It's far better to show that, while you may have preferences, you are flexible and adaptable enough to fit into any team.

WHAT TO INCLUDE

The key is to make an 'educated' guess. Use every resource to try and find out what kind of company, department and team culture you would be joining if you did get this job. Try:

- ▶ speaking to someone who works, or used to work, for the company
- ▶ talking to a customer or supplier of the company
- ▶ obtaining inside information from the recruitment consultant
- ▶ the company website
- ▶ blogs, forums and other Internet postings
- ▶ company press releases, news reports or other public documents.

Once you know the kind of person they are likely to be looking for, it is easier to position yourself as an attractive option. Do you fit with their team culture? Will you work in a style that they encourage?

KEEP TO THE POINT

If you can answer yes, your overall work style or personality fits their typical profile, then find two or three examples of how you have successfully worked in this way for other employers. Keep it relevant (just those examples) and under a minute.

If no, look for those specific ways in which you *would* fit in with their team, and focus only on those.

Specific example – if you know you're a good fit

'From my research, it sounds as if you're a company that likes to look at things differently, and that's exactly what I bring to a team.

'My skills as a designer mean I love brainstorming and like to consider problems from several angles at once, often seeing patterns where others can't.

'Your team also sounds very commercially oriented, which is a good match with my finance background and suits my desire to work on concrete rather than abstract tasks.'

'I enjoy working as part of a team and, because most of my work is project-based, I'm flexible, having experience playing different roles in many different teams.

'My ability to build rapport with team mates quickly has proved really useful for short-term projects, while also helping me to work productively in the long term. I can also work autonomously to complete my own tasks before feeding these back into the group.

'All the key projects in my CV have been the product of successful teamwork.'

LENGTH

One minute is plenty for starters.

LOGIC

Mention the research you've done into the company or team if you've done some. Base the first part of your answer on what you know they want, and the second part on evidence of your successful past teamwork.

Question 12: How do you like to be managed?

Also comes dressed as:

- ▶ 'What would your boss say about you?'
- ▶ 'What would your ideal manager be like?'
- ▶ 'Describe the worst boss you've had.'
- ▶ 'Who's the best/most inspiring manager you've ever worked for?'

WHY IS IT BEING ASKED?

This is very similar to the teamwork question, except focusing on how you like to be managed instead. If the person interviewing you is going to be your manager, this is a very loaded question – how you really like to be managed could be completely in line with their own approach, or the total opposite.

COMMON MISTAKES

Being too prescriptive with your answer, even if you know for a fact what the interviewer would be like as a manager. You will come across as inflexible and therefore difficult to manage if you lay it out too boldly in black and white.

Talking about what you *don't* like is another common error. It makes you sound like a complainer. Even if you're asked a negatively phrased question about your worst-ever boss, bring it quickly round to positive aspects that you *do* like.

WHAT TO INCLUDE

Unless you'll only consider working for someone who manages you in a particular way, a 'horoscope answer' is best here: one that appears to give specifics, but is in fact universal enough to apply to pretty much anyone who hears it. There are many characteristics that are generally considered good in a manager, including (but not limited to):

▶ inspirational/motivational
▶ clear vision
▶ leads by example
▶ develops their staff
▶ calm
▶ able to delegate
▶ trusts staff to get their work done
▶ approachable.

So if you're asked to recall or describe a good manager, or say how you like to be managed, you're on fairly safe ground if you include one or two positive aspects from the above list. Likewise, if you're asked about the negative aspects of an imaginary manager, reverse one or two of these positives and briefly mention those, but move on to the positives very quickly.

Insight

If you're answering the negative question about a 'real' former boss, make sure you only mention one or at most two bad things, then drop in some big positives for balance. That way you won't come across as a nightmare employee who constantly slates their manager or other people – even if you think that it's fully justified in this case!

KEEP TO THE POINT

Stay focused on your preferences and keep them suitably general. Don't get sidetracked into excessive detail about why you hated a particular boss and justify it by saying that no one else liked them either.

Example – ideal boss

'I think a really good manager helps you to place your work in context, so you can relate to the company's objectives and understand how you make a difference. I find that really motivating. My ideal boss would also be even-tempered when under pressure, and have a good sense of humour, so I can really enjoy working with them.'

Example – worst boss

'I like managers who delegate well, so I can use my initiative to get the job done. I'm always happy to have input from my manager at the start of a project, to agree clear expectations and targets, and I like then being left to get on with the job. I did have one manager who was unable to stop herself from micromanaging; although the upside was that I learned a lot about how she thought and worked, which helped me to step up into her role when she went on maternity leave.'

LENGTH

Half a minute should be plenty, so keep your comments very brief. If you take your full minute, you could risk sounding too prescriptive.

LOGIC

Ensure you start and finish on a positive note. For negatively phrased questions, start your answer with positives, mention the one or two negatives briefly, then finish up with more positives. A sandwich of optimism, if you like.

Question 13: Can you explain this gap in your CV?

Ouch. No coincidence that this is number 13 in the list. Its many close relatives include:

▶ 'What happened in June 2007, then?'
▶ 'Can you tell me more about February to May 2009, as it isn't clear from your CV?'

WHY IS IT BEING ASKED?

Probably because you left a gap on your CV. If you think carefully about your CV when you write it, this question shouldn't come as a surprise, if it comes up at all. Filling CV gaps with well-chosen words can help them appear less interesting than other, stronger aspects of your CV. If you do still get quizzed, it should be from a more positive starting point.

Employers are suspicious about anyone who hasn't had a continuous work history. Perhaps it means you are a high-risk employee prone to long periods of illness; maybe you got fired and are trying to cover it up; you might have left your high-pressure job on the spur of the moment and later regretted it, because you didn't have anything else lined up.

No one wants to hire someone who can't perform, who will run away at the first sign of stress, or whom no one else wanted – so interviewers will often latch onto CV gaps.

COMMON MISTAKES

One common mistake is assuming this might not be asked, and therefore not having a story ready to explain your gap (or gaps) in a positive light. Another is not rehearsing your story sufficiently. You need to look (and feel) comfortable, positive and sincere rather than embarrassed, or insincere, or guilty. Even if you don't feel that worried about a gap in your CV, not practising your answer makes it more likely that you could sound dishonest or defensive.

WHAT TO INCLUDE

Just expand on the positive gap description in your CV. The more positive you can be, the better.

Redundancy can be made to sound more positive by focusing on the training courses you attended, any languages you learned, or the skills you gained as a volunteer during the time you weren't in paid employment. A period of illness could be glossed over by pointing out that you've fully regained your health, or have since worked full time (or in a physical job) with no issues. (For more details, read the section on 'honest spin' in *Get That Job with the Right CV*, another title in the Teach Yourself series.)

KEEPING TO THE POINT

The reason behind the gap should be the briefest part of your answer. What really counts is what you did with your time during the gap, what you learned or gained from your time out of paid work.

Insight

The more you practise talking positively about what happened during any gaps, the more positively you will start to think about them. When you feel positive, it's a lot easier to convince an interviewer to feel the same way.

Example

'After I'd spent about six months working for Ego, Maniac & Self Ltd, a small City firm, I realized the way the company worked was at odds with my integrity. Leaving seemed the best option, and the next day I began researching sales opportunities with larger companies, focusing on those with strong principles.

'I identified two suitable opportunities within the same group quite quickly, underwent interviews and assessments, and ended up with my pick of both jobs. I chose the one with the most potential for progression, but then waited five or six weeks more because the position only became fully available when the existing jobholder started maternity leave. It meant we had plenty of time for a great handover, though; I was fully up to speed before she left.'

LENGTH

Keep it to under a minute. You may well be asked further questions based on your answer, but it should still be brief.

Stay consistent with your story and remember to focus on the positive elements.

Question 14: Do you handle stress/pressure well?

Other ways of asking the same thing:

▶ 'Are you really going to be able to cope with this job?'
▶ 'How do you change when you're under pressure?'
▶ 'How would others say stress/pressure affects you?'

WHY IS IT BEING ASKED?

An interviewer is looking for proof with this question – proof that you can handle pressure, ideally with some examples of when and how you've coped well with stressful situations.

COMMON MISTAKES

Following the leading question. Asking about how you change when under pressure, or when you are affected by it, is a leading question. Whosoever perspective you answer from, this kind of phrasing sets up your answer to start with an admission: that yes, you *do* change when under pressure. Once you have acknowledged that, it's almost impossible not to give details of *how* you change.

Avoid a full disclosure approach, such as:

▶ 'Yes, I turn into a complete wreck and start double-checking everyone else's work.'
▶ 'I'm fine for about a week, then I burst into tears – but I'm fine again after a cry.'
▶ 'My stress only shows at home; I get pretty grumpy, so my relationships never tend to last long. But I never let it affect work.'

WHAT TO INCLUDE

Think carefully about any changes you wish to own up to, and how strongly you want to state them. Try to give them an upside, too. Changes like...

- ▶ 'I become quieter so I can concentrate on my work.'
- ▶ 'I start missing lunch and working through so I have time to double-check things.'
- ▶ 'My colleagues say they can only tell when I'm stressed because I stop my usual banter.'

…are all relatively benign, and not extreme.

If your opinion is that you don't change at all when you're under pressure, or that pressure enhances your performance, then avoid the leading element and just say so. If you do this, make sure you still have a couple of examples to support your claims.

KEEPING TO THE POINT

Refer only to work examples – don't mention home. Refer to school work, voluntary work or work experience if you have no work history yet.

Example

'I don't really suffer from stress; if anything, pressure gives me an edge. I mentioned earlier that I like a challenge, so anything that increases the level of challenge makes me all the more determined to raise my game. You'll see from my CV I've held a number of pressurized roles: some involved working to tight weekly deadlines, while others were more complex projects with many milestones. Never missing one of those deadlines became a matter of pride for me, rather than a source of stress.'

LENGTH

If you're admitting a reaction to stress, keep it as short as possible.

If you're saying you have no reaction to stress or it's a very weak one, you can take closer to a minute if you need to.

LOGIC

Back up whatever answer you give with an example – and keep one up your sleeve.

ALTERNATIVE METHODS

The interviewer could also ask this question (or a follow-up question) in a way that puts you under pressure, so they can observe how you really do react. For example: 'What would you say/do if I said this interview has gone pretty badly/you haven't impressed me at all so far?'

The intent of the question is to find out how resilient you are, so the style might be very confrontational. Be careful to restrain your instinctive emotional reaction and, if you claim that pressure doesn't affect you in the slightest, make sure it's actually true.

Example

'Obviously I'd be disappointed, but my priority would be to understand why you felt that way and to see if I could address any points you raised. My sole aim is for you to finish this interview with the right impression of me as someone who can do this job well and really wants it.'

Question 15: Where would you like your career to go next year/in five years' time?

Also couched as:

- ▶ 'What's your next step after this one?'
- ▶ 'What job do you envisage yourself doing in three years' time?'
- ▶ 'Why will this job help you progress in your career?'
- ▶ 'Will you still want to work for us in ten years' time?'
- ▶ 'How long would you intend staying in this role/with this company?'

WHY IS IT BEING ASKED?

However it's phrased, the interviewer would like to believe that you're applying for this job for a reason, not because it's your only last-ditch option but because it somehow fits with your grand plan. They also want to assess whether you intend to stick around long – both in the job and in the company – or whether it's a temporary stepping stone and you'll have left within the year.

....

Insight

Recruitment is an expensive process, so although most companies acknowledge that people generally won't want to stay in the same role for life, they'd be happier hiring someone who shows intent to develop within the company rather than a candidate who will turn up, get what they want, then disappear.

COMMON MISTAKES

Not thinking through where you might go from this job or how it will help you get there. If you're attending an interview for your very first job, you may feel particularly uncertain or want to keep your options open to see which aspects of work you enjoy most. However, that's no excuse for not thinking (and ideally talking) these things through before you get to interview. You will still need to have a coherent logic to why you're applying for this role and what you'd like to work towards. There is no excuse for not having at least thought things through.

Ill-conceived ambition is another turn-off. For example:

Q: *Where do you see yourself in five years' time?*

A: *Doing your job.*

You might think this is a fair enough response and shows some mettle, but watch how you do it. Openly saying you want your interviewer's job can be risky, as you might come across as arrogant. It could look as if you haven't thought about your own career path so are 'borrowing' theirs.

You definitely need a ready answer if the interviewer should then ask which skills you're aiming to develop in order to do their job one day. If you haven't done your research and know exactly what they do and how this role can help prepare you for that, you could end up looking stupid.

Insight

If you do say you're after the interviewer's role, make sure they are definitely the manager of the team you're hoping to join. Believing you're talking to the sales director and saying you'd like their job in ten years' time will get you nowhere if their reply is: 'Oh? Well, if you really want to be a personnel manager I suggest you apply for a job in HR.'

WHAT TO INCLUDE

If you don't have a five-year plan, now's the time to start thinking about one. It doesn't have to be perfect, and you don't have to stick to it religiously if you do get the job – you're entitled to change your mind anytime – but it should make logical sense. Try talking to your manager or more senior people in your current company or industry to discuss what your next theoretical move could be. If not, you could do some online research to look at typical career paths, opportunities for progression and other vacancies within the company.

Once you've done that, think about the kinds of skills you will need to get into the position you want in five years' time. Will you need: sales skills; management experience; better communication; experience in logistics? Whatever you need, ensure the role and company you are applying for will help you develop at least one of those key skills you've identified – that way what you're wanting to do now fits perfectly with what you're wanting to do in future.

KEEPING TO THE POINT

Your five-year plan might change often (whose doesn't?) but you don't need to say that now. Don't allow yourself to get sidetracked by alternative career paths you might also consider. Once you've shaped your plan, stick to talking about that.

If you have an ambition, make sure it's a well-thought-through one, and that you know how you could possibly get from your current position to your goal.

Whatever your answer, don't miss a chance to sell yourself and your skills again.

Example – first timer

'I'm drawn to retail because my biggest strength lies in dealing with people: I believe it's all about working as a team to give customers amazing service. But I also want a career where I can make the most of my numeracy, and I think being good with numbers will really help once I'm in a position to be monitoring sales, analysing promotional activity or measuring profitability.

'Whether it's realistic to think I could be a store manager with this company in ten years' time, I'm not sure yet – but that's my ultimate goal. In this role, my aim will be to give the best customer service I can, while developing the basic leadership skills and retail experience for my next step.'

Example – mid-career

'In ten years' time I'd like to be a production manager, possibly sooner if I've gained enough leadership skill and experience.

'That's why I'm so keen on this job. I've proved I can perform excellently, by helping to improve line efficiency and flexibility by over 15 per cent, but this role will also stretch me because of your plan to introduce so much new technology. While becoming familiar with that technology, I would focus on developing my leadership skills and hopefully progressing from team leader to supervisor, once I've completed my project management qualification.

'By being exposed to brand-new technology from the start, and with the encouragement you say you give employees to move between your five sites to gain experience, I can see my career path developing really well within your company.'

Example – career switcher

'It may sound bold, but in ten years' time I'd like to be a Michelin-starred chef. I think it's a realistic time frame for the amount of learning I have to do.

'As you've seen, my technical skills are already very strong, gained by working part-time in a high-quality restaurant. Having been an accountant in the hotel and leisure sector, my commercial understanding is sound, my organizational skills are strong, and the senior business positions and junior kitchen positions I've held show that I manage well under pressure.

'This role feels like the perfect chance for me to contribute all my skills, passion and commitment while learning how to balance the commercial aspects of kitchen, menu and staff with delivering an exquisite customer experience.'

LENGTH

One minute should be plenty for this answer, but you still need to give it some detailed thought in case you are questioned further on it.

LOGIC

Ensure you know the steps you might take and skills you'll need to gain at each step to reach your five-year or ten-year goal.

Be consistent, stick to talking about the same plan for as long as you're interviewing at this company – don't let it change into something new in a second or third interview.

Further common questions

In this chapter you will learn about:
- *the next most commonly asked questions and some popular incarnations of them*
- *how to deal with them constructively.*

Question 16: How do you rate yourself as an employee?

WHY IS IT BEING ASKED?

Because it is (or should be, when answered properly) another easy way for an interviewer to get a potted summary of what you're all about. They aren't asking in the context of a specific role, or specific work experience, but as a worker in general. It's far easier to let candidates display their plus points this way than to deduce them from different answers.

COMMON MISTAKES

Being too vague. This sounds like a fairly general question, but the answer should NOT be equally general, as, for example, in 'Pretty good all round, really.'·

Just giving yourself a mark out of ten – don't do this without explaining why.

Assuming that you can't answer the question because you've never had a job before; you can still talk about your transferable qualities and say this is what would shape you as an employee.

WHAT TO INCLUDE

The question doesn't ask about specifics, but it's still a great chance to highlight how well you meet the softer skills in the job advert: those that relate more to personality traits than your specific work experience. So tailor your answer to the job advert; if it is sketchy, or there isn't one (you are applying speculatively), then you can talk about qualities that are considered positive by most employers.

Are you enthusiastic by nature? Curious? Willing to learn? Flexible? Perhaps you show perseverance, tenacity and determination to get the job done. Maybe, in addition to your professional skills, your biggest plus point is the ambition that drives you to excel at everything you try? Is loyalty your biggest asset? Or is it that you've got a great sense of humour yet are still professional?

Whatever aspects you choose to focus on, stay scientific: prove your claims. When it comes to soft skills, that can seem more difficult, but it's still possible. Anything related to working over and above the standard (preparing a presentation over a weekend, staying late to finish something) can be used to show motivation, commitment, dedication, determination or tenacity.

Insight

Proof of softer skills, especially harder-to-define ones such as a sense of humour, is often better given as a testimonial: recounting something another person has said about you. You could say just about anything, but it can still be powerful evidence, particularly if you provide a name and job title to go with that testimonial.

Example

'I'm a very motivational employee. In my last appraisal, my manager said that aside from hitting my targets, my greatest value came from lightening the atmosphere in R&D without being unprofessional or inappropriate. He said that my sense of humour, enthusiasm and approachability were key factors in making it a nicer place to work, and this was borne out by feedback from all my colleagues. I took that as the highest compliment; it was this that prompted me to start looking for a role like this, where I can have a bigger influence on morale and productivity, while developing management skills.'

Question 17: What do team members say about you?

WHY IS IT BEING ASKED?

To establish whether you're aware of, or have thought about, what your colleagues think about you and your work. Being sensitive to the impact you have on others, being able to read their non-verbal feedback, and welcoming other types of feedback, are social skills that are highly prized in employees.

Feedback from colleagues often focuses more on soft skills and personal qualities than on work performance, although that's not to say you can't talk about both.

COMMON MISTAKES

Mentioning something negative. Never raise negative issues yourself.

Assuming this question wouldn't be followed up with 'And what would they say that is not so complimentary?' Make sure you think about this part (like Question 7: 'What are your weaknesses?') and have one or two things to mention before coming back to positives.

WHAT TO INCLUDE

This can be answered similarly to Question 6: 'What are your strengths?' or 'What are your strengths, in the eyes of others?', although it would be good to have your proof based at least partly on testimonials to give it credibility.

Alternatively you could draw from Question 16 above, which may well be largely testimonial-based anyway.

Example

Please refer to the example answers to Questions 6 and 16, in Chapter 10 and this chapter respectively.

Question 18: What makes you angry at work?

You may also meet this in similar guises to the following:

- ▶ 'What irritates you in the workplace?'
- ▶ 'What type of person/situation brings out the worst in you?'

WHY IS IT BEING ASKED?

This is such a leading question. It implies that you get angry, irritated or display other undesirable traits while at work, and it is encouraging you not only to own up to it but to explain exactly what sets you off.

COMMON MISTAKES

Not starting by refuting the interviewer's assumption. If you start by saying what makes you angry, then backtrack to say that it's never a problem at work, it sounds as if you're trying to cover up your natural tendency to get angry. Allowing yourself to be drawn by silence or a raised eyebrow. Once you've given your answer, don't under any circumstances feel obliged to throw anything else into the ring. Displaying anger, about anything, at any point during the interview.

WHAT TO INCLUDE

If you want the interviewer to understand that you are a laid-back, unflappable person when at work, then answer by clearly refuting their suggestion.

Keep it nice and short so it doesn't sound like you're being defensive or making excuses.

Example

'I don't remember ever having been angry at work. That is despite dealing with stressful situations and plenty of seemingly unreasonable customers, so I'd have to say – not a lot makes me angry. Nothing I've experienced or could imagine experiencing, anyway.'

Example

'I'm not easily irritated. I know some of my colleagues find it hard to deal with some of our more arrogant and demanding clients, but I always look for something to like in every person I deal with. By focusing on that, other people's behaviour never seems to get to me.'

Question 19: With hindsight, would you choose a different career path?

Alternatives include:

- ▶ 'Looking back, do you now wish you'd chosen a different degree course?'
- ▶ 'Now that you're applying for a job in this field, don't you wish you'd studied different subjects?'

WHY IS IT BEING ASKED?

This is a bit like asking if you have any regrets (see Question 8 in Chapter 10). The interviewer is trying to uncover past mistakes you may feel you have made. They may be looking for evidence that you act impulsively then regret it later.

COMMON MISTAKES

Agreeing and saying yes, you wish you'd done everything differently. While it's all well and good to admit to mistakes and learn from them, you can also open a can of worms – and if you've already admitted to making mistakes in answer to other questions, it could start to look as if you make rather a lot of mistakes.

You do also need to show you are capable of making informed decisions. At most a partial acknowledgement that you might have reached a goal a little quicker if you'd done something differently would be acceptable, though.

WHAT TO INCLUDE

Show that you had a plan then, and you have a plan now. Rather than saying you wish your choices had been different, it's better to say you're happy with the decisions you made when you made them, because they made sense based on the information or goals you had at that time.

If a decision you made later turned out to have a negative impact, because of a change in your circumstances or your goals, then your response should not be that you wish for things to have been different, but that you adapted to those changes with your later decisions.

It's a negative question but a great chance to reinforce your strong points.

Example – straight refusal

'No, I don't regret studying Psychology at university even though I didn't go on to become a psychologist. I chose a degree that I would really enjoy studying, which would show my ability to learn, analyse and argue at an advanced level, and where some of the things I learned – especially about social psychology – could potentially be useful in a work context.

'I loved my time at university, came away with a First and have applied my understanding to numerous roles since then.'

Example – minor admission

'No, I don't wish I'd studied different subjects as my education stood me in good stead for the career I wanted in administration. It was only during my second job for a much larger firm that I was exposed to finance and discovered I had such an aptitude for it. I then studied for and passed Maths A Level in my spare time, so that I could get sponsored for my CIMA accountancy exams. I don't feel as if I've missed anything because of it.

'In hindsight, if I'd joined Harris & Ford Global Ventures earlier, I may have advanced sooner, but my time at Clooney & Clooney was such a great introduction to working life. It taught me great interpersonal skills, clear communication and, above all, time management – without which I wouldn't be where I am now.'

'It might seem as if I'd like to turn the clock back, but what's right for me now is different to what was right for me years ago, so I feel I made the right decisions. I wanted to work with people, travel internationally, build relationships and work with advanced technology. My Physics degree led neatly into a career selling forensic laboratory equipment, which gave me everything I had wanted.

'As a respected salesperson at the top of my field, I feel I've achieved everything I set out to. My desire to now teach sciences at secondary school follows naturally from enthusiasm for the subject and my proven talent for explaining difficult concepts to non-technical people. I feel comfortable talking to any type or size of audience, including children.

'I appreciate the salary doesn't compare but I earned well during my time in sales, and my priority now is a role where I can have a tangible impact on other people's lives.'

Question 20: What sort of suggestions or improvements have you made at work?

WHY IS IT BEING ASKED?

You're being invited to show whether you can think creatively about problem solving and making improvements. Interviewers are more impressed by someone who has seen an opportunity to do something better and spoken up, than they are by someone who just keeps their head down and does the job they're given.

COMMON MISTAKES

Saying you can't think of any. Find one. Every little improvement counts, whether you encouraged people to send more emails instead of faxes to save phone costs, whether you suggested introducing coffee mugs and kettles instead of using paper cups and hot drinks machines to save on drinks costs and disposable items; think of something you did that made a difference. If it's your first job interview, think about something you've made a difference to at school, in activities after school, even at home.

WHAT TO INCLUDE

It's good to show you not only have ideas but also that you use your initiative to put them forward, or better still act upon them. Best of all is if those ideas have a measurable positive impact. Having two or more examples ready shows that it is a standard way of working for you, rather than a one-off.

Insight

Your examples should show a measurable benefit – i.e., why you suggested the change in the first place. Did you save man hours, reduce wastage, raise quality, increase sales or profit, reduce mistakes, improve cash flow, boost morale, retain a valuable client, increase productivity, limit damages? Even if it's hard to measure, try to estimate it in real terms.

Example

'In the contact lens call centre I worked in, different teams handled different types of query: new business in one area, accounting queries in another, complaints in another. I noticed soon after joining the new business team that each team had a very different atmosphere – we were generally busy and quite enthusiastic, accounts spent a lot of time chatting, while complaints seemed stressed and tended to lose people regularly.

'My idea was that it would be better if all calls were shared with everyone, so we all had a chance to deal with 'good' as well as 'bad' calls. At first our manager was reluctant, so I asked if we could do a pilot test with one person from each team. It worked brilliantly.

'So, we became one team. The atmosphere improved, as the work was more interesting and less stressful, and staff turnover went down. And, as an unexpected bonus, holiday cover became far easier to organize.'

Question 21: Would you say you are successful? / How successful are you?

WHY IS IT ASKED?

This is a bit like the 'How do you rate yourself as an employee?' question, but much more specific. The interviewer wants to gauge how highly you think of yourself and whether you can justify it.

COMMON MISTAKES

Sounding overconfident or arrogant. No one wants to admit to being mediocre, but it can easily go the other way.

Thinking that because you haven't had a job before you can't have been successful.

WHAT TO INCLUDE

The best way to answer this question is to keep it concrete, with proof. Talking positively won't make you sound arrogant if you support it with facts in an objective way.

It's another great opportunity to draw attention to the achievements you want the interviewer to remember. If you haven't mentioned any yet, here's your chance; and if you have, you can refer to them again much more briefly and perhaps add a further example.

Example – with career experience

'Yes, I'd say I've been successful as an events planner. In ten years I've gone from arranging small parties for up to 30 guests to project-managing events attended by hundreds. My client list has grown from ten individuals to numerous international corporations, and I'm responsible for a turnover of nearly £2 million, with good profitability. I feel a great way to build on this success would be to join your company and grow your business even larger, while gaining experience in specialist channels.'

'My time at school was quite successful – I left with B and C grades across a wide range of subjects. Then came my real success: I was one of just two people chosen from nearly 60 applicants for an apprenticeship at the local bus company, which is still the best training a motor engineer can get. I finished my apprenticeship with really good comments from the workshop manager, and gained all my City & Guilds qualifications, so I think I've been as successful as I can be in reaching this point. I'd like to build on that in a company with a reputation like Hamburgini, so my next success would be getting this job.'

Question 22: What have you done to improve your knowledge in the last year?

WHY IS IT BEING ASKED?

Employers like employees who want to learn and develop. For nurses, continuing professional development is a mandatory part of the job if you wish to keep your registration. For jobs that don't have this as a requirement, it's still highly desirable.

COMMON MISTAKES

We've all done it at some point; sat back and wondered what on earth we've done this year. That's fine, but don't give the interviewer any reason to wonder the same thing.

Answering passively, as in: 'My employer sent me on a course.' The question is about what *you* have done to improve your knowledge, not what your employer has told you to do, so ensure you include a comment about how proactive you were.

WHAT TO INCLUDE

If you can, any 'knowledge improvement' activities you mention should relate to the job at hand. Mention relevant skills training, or experience you've gained by taking on additional responsibility at work. Volunteer work, online courses and reading up on a subject are other good ways to improve your knowledge. Just make sure that what you mention is completely true, in case you are questioned in more depth on the details.

If this is your first interview, don't forget to talk about any job shadowing or work experience you did while at school or university. This may not be directly relevant to this job, but it still counts as knowledge you've gained and you may have learned some skills that would be transferable to this job.

If you're still at application stage with any jobs, think about whether it could increase your employability if you do some training or gain knowledge in another way – even reading a relevant book. If so, do it sooner rather than later and try to make it all relevant in some way to the roles you're applying for.

Example

'Once I decided I wanted to work in commodities buying, I started reading up on this commodity and watching the markets. I've been following cocoa futures for almost a month now, and I've learned so much already. I know I'll need to learn your systems as well, but I am really glad I have the basics: I've become familiar with the different varieties of cocoa and where it's grown, who the growers are and how the whole trading process works. All that has made me even keener on working for Barrs Confectionery in this role.'

Question 23: Are you applying for other jobs?

WHY IS IT ASKED?

Sometimes this sort of question is used more earnestly at a second or third interview. This is when the interviewer is trying to gauge how serious you are about wanting to join their company, how soon they will need to act, and where in the pecking order they are likely to be if you receive more than one job offer.

Insight

Interviewers know that you'll probably be applying to other companies, especially if you're a first-time job seeker or currently out of work. Few people have the luxury of being a serial applicant, waiting for a rejection note before moving on to the next. Just don't make it look as if you've fired CVs out with a shotgun, hoping one will hit a target.

If you're at final interview stage, they may try to find out in detail what you're being offered and by whom so that they can, if they want to, match or exceed that offer. As with any negotiation, it doesn't pay to give away information for nothing. If they ask for details of your other offers, don't feel scared to ask if they are making you a formal offer and, if so, what it might be.

COMMON MISTAKES

Answering: 'Dur... what do *you* think? Of course I am.'

WHAT TO INCLUDE

It's no bad thing for an interviewer to be aware that you are applying elsewhere, for similar roles, if that makes logical sense and supports what you've told them. It could pay to be a little elusive, though. You're not obliged to say who the other employers are, unless you want to. However, if you're quite some way along the recruitment process somewhere else and you want to encourage this interviewer to decide quickly, it may be worth revealing that much at least.

The main content of your answer should focus on you, not on other employers.

Example

'As I'm looking for my first job, I have sent out a few other applications: I'm keen on working in this field but particularly this opportunity. I believe my technical drawing skills and CAD experience would be of use to you straight away, and I'm really hoping I get this job too because your next packaging project is something I would find really interesting.'

Question 24: Do you know anyone who works here?

WHY IS IT ASKED?

This is quite an innocent-seeming question and sometimes it can be just that: a polite enquiry.

Or it could be a query because of company policy. Find out if it's acceptable to have relatives or people in a relationship working together in this organization. Some employers prefer relationships between employees to be based purely on working co-operation, so that business decisions cannot be influenced by personal considerations. Other employers actively welcome people known to, and rated highly by, existing employees – they could be a safer hire than someone nobody knows.

COMMON MISTAKES

The only way you can go wrong with this answer is to lie. If you know company policy does not allow for relationships between employees, then the fact that you're living with the deputy production manager is relevant and will be uncovered – if not today, then in future. If it's a large corporation and you can't guarantee that you don't somehow know someone who works here, you can always use the classic: 'No – at least, not that I'm aware of.'

WHAT TO INCLUDE

Tell the truth and make it short. You have absolutely no reason to hide anything or feel uneasy: it really is a straightforward question.

Example

'Yes, my brother-in-law works in the finance department; it was he who first recommended this opportunity.'

Question 25: What is your philosophy towards work?

WHY IS IT ASKED?

This is used to try and establish 'fit' – will the way you work mesh well with the way the company likes its employees to work?

COMMON MISTAKES

Being too prescriptive with your answer. If your philosophy towards work is very eccentric, or very selfish, then it won't seem attractive to your future employer.

WHAT TO INCLUDE

Your philosophy towards work is what role work plays in your life and how you approach it. It's a bit like the old cliché about whether you live to work, or whether you work to live.

Most employers will be keener to hire someone who puts work first, is committed to their employer, and will go above and beyond their daily duties if there is a need. Ideally, they want someone who takes pride in their work and gets satisfaction from it, because people tend to try harder at things they enjoy.

Conversely, if you say that work is simply a vehicle for earning money so you can do all the things you really love in life, then it could cast doubt on where your priorities lie. Are you really bothered about working in this company or this role, or are you just after anything that pays the bills?

As always, the most attractive candidate is usually someone who achieves a balance – who works hard but also plays hard. Someone who burns out from working all the time won't perform their best and could end up being a long-term liability. The person who puts in their all when they're at work but also knows how to have a life outside of it is likely to be a more rounded individual, possibly with a wider range of useful skills.

Example

'As I spend most of my waking time at work, it's important that I enjoy some aspect of it – exactly what that is depends on the job. In this role, it's the variety that really appeals, and the chance to develop new skills over the long term.

'Anything that presents me with a challenge gives me satisfaction, and I am always willing to put in extra time and effort at work to see results. But I also believe that it's important to have a life outside work; I really enjoy kite-surfing, so I take every opportunity I can to get down to the coast and stretch myself in a completely different way in my free time. It keeps me fit and I find some time away from a work problem often gives me a better perspective when I get back.'

Question 26: Are you willing to relocate?

WHY IS IT ASKED?

This question is pretty straightforward, although it may come up for several reasons:

- You're applying for a job based further than commuting distance from your current address. So, if you want this job, they want to know if you will move for it and how quickly you can do that.
- There's a plan to move the company or division to a different location next year – they want to know if you would relocate if you had already started in the job.
- It can be a general question for the future, to see if you are likely to be flexible and go anywhere the company wants you to as part of your career development.
- To test whether you were telling the truth on your CV.

COMMON MISTAKES

Answering yes when you mean no. There's a good chance an experienced interviewer will spot a lie – that's often why this question is asked, even though you've already put 'willing to relocate' on your CV. But, besides, if the job requires relocation why are you applying for it?

Saying 'never'. Even if you're not keen on the idea of relocating now, what if this company offered you a dream promotion in a year or two – do you really want to rule out future options now?

WHAT TO INCLUDE

Answer as honestly as you can.

Obviously if you're applying to do a job based a long way away, you would need to move. In this case it may help if you've already looked at places where you're interested in living, and can explain how soon you'd be able to start work if offered the job.

If there's no mention or need for relocation based on the current vacancy, and the relocation question is a hypothetical one to establish your future flexibility, then there's nothing wrong with saying you'd certainly be willing to consider it for the right role.

You might want to place a constraint on that by saying which areas you'd consider relocating to – within the UK perhaps, or further afield.

Example – will relocate for this role

'Yes, I'm more than happy to relocate as I'm really keen on this opportunity. I've already done some research into the local area and like the look of Maidenhead and Taplow, either of which would be nice and close to the office. Selling my flat may take some time, but I've spoken to friends in this area and they'd be happy to rent me a room during the working week – so I'd be able to start as soon as you wanted. If I couldn't sell my flat I'd be equally happy to let it out, and rent locally myself in the long term.'

Example – theoretical relocation question

'I wasn't actively looking to relocate just now, and this opportunity wouldn't require it from what I can see. However, I would certainly consider relocating anywhere within the UK for the right kind of opportunity in future.'

Question 27: Are you able to work overtime/ nights/weekends if required?

WHY IS IT ASKED?

The interviewer may just want to know how keen you are on this job or company. Will you do whatever they ask of you to succeed?

COMMON MISTAKES

It will likely count against you if you give a flat 'No'. Every employer likes to think staff will try to be flexible and put in extra time if there is a real business need for doing so.

A straight 'Yes' can seem suspicious; how many sensible people agree to something without knowing the extent of what they are agreeing to?

Asking immediately what the overtime rate is. Wait until you have a firm job offer before asking for this detail, if it's a job with an hourly rate and overtime is not mentioned in the offer. For a salaried position it's rare that overtime pay would be offered.

WHAT TO INCLUDE

If you genuinely cannot work any overtime then by all means say so, but you could be closing the door on yourself.

A willing, positive answer, coupled with a question to find out the extent of the overtime they have in mind, is probably safest. If they say you'd probably be needed every Saturday for the next year, it might change how you feel about the role or salary on offer.

'I've always been happy to work overtime when the job demands it. I averaged one evening a week for Comfort Foods Ltd when we had a big order going through, and I worked one weekend every month when I was at Delicious Delicacies, so we could do routine cleaning and maintenance on the pastry and custard machines.

'Can I ask how often this position tends to require it? How much warning or choice is there, and does it tend to be nights, weekends, or a mix of both?'

Insight

If you have worked overtime in the past, be sure to mention this – it adds weight to your claim to be willing to work extra hours for this employer.

Question 28: What motivates you?

WHY IS IT ASKED?

This is a positively framed question: it assumes you can be motivated. What the interviewer wants to know is what does the trick for you. They want to know if it's something that they can offer you or if you're unlikely to be motivated by this role.

COMMON MISTAKES

Saying something the employer has no control over, such as: 'Football. When Arsenal are doing well I feel on top of the world, like I can do anything, and it motivates me to achieve my goals at work.' If this is true, your employer can't influence when you'll feel motivated.

WHAT TO INCLUDE

You may, quite simply, be self-motivated. Perhaps you want to do well at anything you turn your hand to, because of the way you are. In theory, that's attractive to an employer: you won't need extra input to keep you performing at 100 per cent. But in reality, self-motivation is only the beginning. Other factors can affect self-motivation, so when answering this question it's worth acknowledging one or two that enhance yours.

If you can, mention things that are related to this job. If the job has fixed targets, perhaps a teaching role, you could say you find measuring your progress towards targets very motivational. If you apply for a sales job with commission, you can safely admit to being motivated by the earnings potential that's linked to success. (If you said this when going for a fixed salary position, however, an interviewer could assume you'd get demotivated over time.) You might also feel enthused by learning new skills, so that having variety in your role or extra training keeps you motivated.

Insight

When being interviewed for your first job, talk about what has motivated you to excel in your studies, sports, music, or whichever area your achievements have been strongest. Working in a team may have spurred you on to achieve more than you would have alone: if you're applying for a team-oriented job, this would be a strong example to give.

Example

'My motivation largely comes from within; I like to perform at my best, no matter what I'm doing, and you'll see from my CV that I've achieved success in academic studies, sports and music. I put that all down to being very self-motivated to do well.

'I'm also very motivated by other people's successes, particularly if they're connected to me. At a recent rugby sevens tournament, I was in the first team and struggling to play well; hearing our second team was winning all their matches spurred me on to better things. So I think a company where successes are openly shared and celebrated would be extra motivation for me.'

Question 29: How do you measure your success?

WHY IS IT ASKED?

It's believed by many interviewers that people who set themselves goals, and monitor their performance against those goals, will be more focused and achieve more than people who float along merely trying hard.

COMMON MISTAKES

Looking puzzled. This question might take you by surprise if you haven't planned or practised an answer, but a blank stare can suggest success isn't important to you or you haven't a clue how to measure it. Not an ideal characteristic for a high-flyer.

Getting too personal with your answer can be a risk. You might appear shallow or materialistic if earning the right salary, living in the right house, driving the right car, holidaying in the right places or wearing the right clothes means success. Maybe approval, recognition, status, respect, happiness, security, quality of life or friendships mean success to you. But this is a job interview, so focus on work as much as you can.

WHAT TO INCLUDE

So, what *do* you measure your success against?

One common way is by comparing yourself with other people's successes, be they colleagues or role models. You can also measure yourself against a fixed benchmark, set targets, people's expectations, or your own expectations.

When explaining how you measure your success, it's an ideal time to talk about some of your past successes – don't miss the selling opportunity. If your work involves achieving set targets, you could measure specifically whether you are selling the expected number of Easter eggs, or generating high enough profit from chocolate chickens, or producing more tonnes of chocolate per hour than you did last year.

You might use career progression as a marker of your success or, if you're commission-based, income. As long as the measure is closely related to what you're trying to achieve, then it's a sound measure of success. If you haven't worked before, give examples based on academic achievement or excellence in leisure activities.

Example – work

'I measure success in how far I go beyond what's expected of me. If I'm set a target, I'm rarely happy just to meet it; it's when I exceed it that I feel like a real success – otherwise I'm basically just doing my job.

'When I was at school, I felt like a success when I achieved grades above my predicted grades. At university, it was getting promoted into the first boat after making the rowing squad. And in my first consulting job, it was saving clients more money than we'd promised them at the start of each project.'

'I've not worked in customer service before, but I'd expect to measure my success based on how satisfied my customers are. If this can't be directly measured, then something related, like how much money they spend with us.

'On paper, my success to date is measured by my exam results – I did really well in the core subjects needed for this job. But for me, success was about excelling in more than one area. Staying competitive at rugby and keeping up my training while also doing well in my exams is what I count as success. It might sound funny but my success at rugby is measured in curry: we celebrate with a curry night whenever we win, and I've eaten out every Saturday since the beginning of September. As a guide to success, that's one I like.'

Question 30: What is your management style?

This kind of question could be asked of almost anything you might do at work; anything where personal style, preferences and beliefs influence your performance and its impact on other people. It could also be phrased as:

- ▶ 'How would you sum up your approach to... your teaching?'
- ▶ 'What is your... staff development ethos?'
- ▶ 'How would you describe your... communication style?'

WHY IS IT ASKED?

The main point of this question is to try and assess if your working style will fit well with the organization you're hoping to join. If you are a relaxed, approachable, operationally involved manager who likes sitting with your team, then taking a management role based in a glass corner office away from your team might be hard to adjust to.

Likewise, if you enjoy working at a clearly identified level in a formal hierarchy, and expect your team to make an appointment with your secretary if they need to discuss anything with you, then an open-plan office where managers sit alongside team members without the 'usual' trappings of management, may be a shock.

Insight

It's not only formal management skills that have an influence and are of interest. Even as a team leader you can influence how other members of your team develop. Coaches can often be found at every level in an organization; everyone has something they're good at that they can help impart to colleagues.

COMMON MISTAKES

As with anything related to style (or preference), being too fixed in what you say. This can suggest you are limited in how you apply your skills and, if your preferences don't match the interviewer's, then you're unlikely to be viewed positively.

WHAT TO INCLUDE

With any skill, the ability to tailor it to your audience is important. That means being adaptable: a one-trick pony will have a shorter future with a company than someone who can change with a changing team or circumstances.

You may naturally gravitate to a relaxed style of management, but don't overstate it: it doesn't mean you would necessarily avoid formal disciplinary procedures if the need arose. A forthright and slightly cynical communication style might be brilliant when working closely with colleagues you know well, whereas you'll need to acknowledge that meetings with senior clients require a more formal communication style.

As for any answer, give examples to demonstrate – ideally two. If your natural preference is in line with the organization you're applying to, make this clear and give a strong example of how it's worked well in the past. But try to present a balanced picture by giving a second example of when you've used a very different style to good effect.

'My management style leans towards the informal. I found at both Analyse Inc. and Consult Inc. that this really helped to build stronger, more united teams with the feeling that "we're all in this together".

'However, informal doesn't mean slack or inviting a lack of respect. I follow a structured approach to monitoring performance, staff appraisal and development, and to disciplinary issues. I'm very clear about what I expect from members of the team, but I maintain a level of informality so that people feel able to approach me at any time.

'One German team member I worked with seemed less comfortable with this management style, and wasn't really gelling with the team, so I started conducting our structured meetings in a more formal way. I also made sure to solicit his feedback during team meetings rather than expecting him to speak up: his contribution improved enormously after that.'

Question 31: Do you have any questions for me?

It's reasonable to assume, whatever your interview, that it's good to ask at least one question at this point because it shows interest and enthusiasm. That is, provided the question hasn't already been answered during this interview, or in material sent to you, or in a former interview.

The focus of these chapters is on answering questions, so for more detailed guidance and ideas on what to ask, please see **Chapter 17: Your own questions.**

12

Behavioural/competency questions

In this chapter you will learn about:
- *the questions that explore how you operate in the workplace – for example, your willingness to take risks*
- *the importance of offering concrete examples as proof.*

Behavioural or competency interviews are often viewed with fear or suspicion, but they're just based on a particular type of question that could come up in *any* interview. This type of question is when you're asked to give an example of how you behaved in a certain way or applied a particular skill or competency in the past.

They demand what you should include in all your answers anyway: proof of your claims, examples of when you showed your skills. Past behaviour is thought to be a good predictor of future behaviour, so questions about what you've actually done should in theory be more useful than other types of question.

Typical question format

Behavioural/competency questions are usually of the type:

- ▶ 'Tell me about a time when you…'
- ▶ 'Describe an example of how you have…'
- ▶ 'Do you…'
- ▶ 'Are you…'

Likely topics

You can often predict which questions will come up. Questions about core skills or competencies listed in the job advert are most likely, then secondary or non-essential skills from the advert, and lastly any other skills or competencies you may mention on your CV.

As a rule, try to prepare at least three examples of when you've used a particular skill or competency to improve an outcome and benefit your employer. It's likely that one will not be enough; even if it is, it never hurts to prepare more. If you have used the Teach Yourself guide to CV writing, you should have several prepared examples of each skill or competency as part of your generic CV. In this case, all you need to do is refamiliarize yourself with these and pick the most suitable three.

Suitable proof

Suitability comes from recentness and relevance.

Recent ideally means within the last year, to indicate that this competency is something you put to good use regularly. Something you did ten years ago might appear to be the strongest example but it's not as relevant or powerful as something you did last week. It could work as a second or third example, though, to show that you've always worked successfully in this way.

Relevance means useful in the job you'll be doing if hired. Many skills and competencies are separate from context: for example, a good leader should be a good leader, whether you work in a metalworking plant, a supermarket or a school. However, your answer could carry extra weight if you show you've used your skills in a similar environment to the one you're hoping to enter.

Question 32: Do you cope well under pressure?

Or...

▶ 'Can you give me an example of a time when you coped well under pressure?'

Please refer back to Question 14 in Chapter 10 for general guidelines on answering this question.

POTENTIAL PROOF

Here's some ideas of examples you could give, to help you think of your own:

- ▶ making a tight deadline
- ▶ calming someone who was angry
- ▶ dealing with a large group of people
- ▶ taking ad hoc questions after a presentation
- ▶ handling a serious complaint
- ▶ making someone redundant
- ▶ negotiating your promotion and pay rise.

Make sure any work-based examples made a positive difference to your job performance or employer. Prioritize any such examples.

If you don't have enough examples from work, or this interview is for your first job, quote examples from outside work:

- ▶ giving first aid to someone
- ▶ taking your final exams
- ▶ scoring a deciding penalty in a football match
- ▶ working for the Samaritans and taking a call from a suicidal person
- ▶ preventing a bar fight
- ▶ passing your driving test in really bad weather / in a car you haven't driven before
- ▶ calmly solving a problem at your best friend's wedding.

Question 33: Do you take the initiative? / Are you a proactive kind of person?

Or...

- ▶ 'Can you describe a time when you've used your initiative/been proactive?'
- ▶ 'And another?' (And another?!)

Employers like employees who don't have to be told what to do all the time. If you see something that should be fixed, improved, solved, or implemented, or you see someone who needs help or a gap that needs to be filled, and you step in and do it yourself (or get the ball rolling, if you're unable to actually do it yourself), then you've used your initiative and been proactive.

POTENTIAL PROOF

▶ You're the only person who understands the computer system inside out and often help colleagues with questions. You decide to document all the main processes and put it on a shared drive for everyone to use, saving everyone time.

▶ You repair machinery in a factory and notice certain parts are often out of stock. This causes shutdowns while parts get couriered at great cost. You start monitoring which parts need replacing and how often, and give the person who orders spares a forecast of what to keep in stock. This reduces delays and saves money.

▶ The toilets are often left in a poor state, notices don't seem to help, and it creates a bad impression for visitors. You suggest a roster where staff members take turns to check and clean the facilities. Now they not only remain tidy for visitors, but there is less mess to clean up because everyone is taking responsibility.

Example

'A colleague ordered 150 posters advertising a special event, but with the wrong date printed on. The white text said 14th instead of 11th April. There was no time to order more. I took one poster and coloured in the 4 so it looked like a 1, and it looked pretty good. With two colleagues, we had all 150 posters ready to be used by the end of the lunch break. The posters weren't wasted and we didn't lose business from not advertising the event.'

Question 34: Are you a team player?

This may also be cast as:

▶ 'Do you work well in teams?'
▶ 'Please describe an occasion when you worked in a team to achieve a goal: what part did you play and would you do anything differently next time?'

▶ 'Tell me about a time when a team project failed: what part did you play and what did you learn from it?'

WHY IS IT ASKED?

Every employer needs people who can work in a team, even if the role you're applying for doesn't demand a lot of teamwork. If you've had even one brief job, your examples should ideally come from the workplace. Volunteer work is also fine. If not, you can mention teamwork in relation to sports, or any group or club activity with a common goal.

Insight

Even the most independent, isolated role still normally involves *some* co-operation or communication with others, so it's important not to discount it. Also, you probably won't stay in this job forever: successful teamwork means you'll be able to work effectively with others whenever needed – now or in future.

COMMON MISTAKES

Not being honest about the part you played in the team. You don't have to be the team or project leader to make a valuable or even essential contribution. What's important is that you understand what you need to contribute, when and how, and that you then do it.

Dwelling on failure. Your emphasis should be, once you've briefly explained how the failure arose, on what you did and how you worked differently to be more successful the next time. That way the interviewer will end up associating you with success, rather than failure.

WHAT TO INCLUDE

When asked about teamwork that was a success, include in your answer a brief summary of...

▶ the purpose of the teamwork/project objective
▶ the team members
▶ what part you played
▶ the timescale involved
▶ factors that influenced success
▶ obstacles that arose and the part you played in overcoming them
▶ how you measured your own progress
▶ why it was deemed a success (how it benefited the company).

Show you are aware of your own skills and strengths. It's important you can put across your knowledge and skills clearly to the team, so these can be taken full advantage of. The roles or actions you take within a team should be appropriate for your capabilities, and you should be able to monitor your progress to stay on track.

Insight

When talking about teamwork that failed, try to pick an example where you clearly understand (and can explain) why things didn't go as well as they could have. Your safest bet is a project affected by external factors beyond your control. If not there is no shame in having failed, only in not learning from the experience. Explain what happened, what you did to help resolve any problems that were caused, and what you learned that would help you avoid similar issues in future.

POTENTIAL PROOF

Team successes are easy to identify: it's anything positive where you didn't work alone. If you're looking at team failure, and are not really sure what went wrong, here are some areas to consider:

- ▶ Team members may not have been used according to their skills. The most talented rugby prop would find it hard to play a winning game if asked to play wing instead.
- ▶ Objectives were not clearly understood or were changed. This may be the project manager's fault but it's best to avoid blaming others if you were not clear on objectives or how to measure your progress – it was your responsibility to clarify.
- ▶ A failure to communicate effectively, at any point in the team project.
- ▶ 'External' factors: a change of direction by management; budget cuts; changes in technology; failure of another team to deliver something essential to yours; or a disastrous event (e.g. damage to infrastructure or equipment, absence of key people through long-term illness).

Example – positive

'I worked as part of a team to arrange the office Christmas event. I've got lots of contacts from previously working in the hospitality industry so I volunteered to secure, book and decorate the venue within budget, while three colleagues managed the theme, the entertainment and the catering. We worked really well together, having regular meetings and covering for each other during holidays. I managed to negotiate a great venue next to the river, and get a boat ride thrown in for free, which freed up extra budget for entertainment. Feedback from the event was that it was the best Christmas party ever, and we underspent the budget so there's even more to play with next year.'

Question 35: Are you motivated / easily motivated?

Or...

▶ 'How would I get the best out of you?'
▶ 'Give me an example of when you've been really motivated?'
▶ 'And another?' (And another?!)

Please refer back to Question 28 in Chapter 11 for advice on answering motivation questions.

WHAT TO INCLUDE

If you claim to be a motivated person, have more than one example ready to talk about. Explain when and where, why and how motivated you were, and how much effort you put in above and beyond what was expected. Make sure you include the outcome of your motivation, namely, what benefit this achieved for your employer.

Example

'I'm very self-motivated, particularly when faced with a challenge. In my last sales job there was a chance to win a huge equipment tender. Despite intense competition I felt it was a realistic goal so I ran as many trials as I could, promoting the product and our after-sales service. It meant an extra visit to that company nearly every day in the month before the tender, without letting other business slide.

'In the final negotiations, run by my manager, we were level on pricing with another supplier – but got selected because of the user support the trials had gained.

'We won the order, worth over £120,000, the biggest single order the company had ever received.

'My commission was cut because the sell price was discounted, but I was still delighted with the achievement. My manager even framed a copy of the order and presented it to me at year end.'

Question 36: Would you say you were creative?

This will very probably followed by:

▶ 'Why? Give me an example of when you've shown creativity.'

WHY IS IT ASKED?

In a work context, creative means someone who thinks about things differently, makes connections that aren't obvious, takes something out of context or looks at solving a problem in a different way to normal. Creativity is subjective, which makes it hard to measure. If someone looks at you and says 'Oh, I would never have thought of it like that/doing it that way,' then to them, you will appear creative.

COMMON MISTAKES

Interpreting the question as asking if you are artistic. This refers to a different kind of creativity.

Thinking it's not that important. Creativity helps companies gain a competitive advantage, helps them to make leaps of design or efficiency; it's a very sought-after skill.

Insight

You may hear the following kinds of overused corporate jargon referring to encouraging creativity at work:

▶ 'We need to think outside the box.'
▶ 'Let's do some blue-sky thinking.'
▶ 'How about a brainstorming session?'

These phrases and many more like them echo far beyond American shores, but try to avoid falling into the trap of using them yourself.If you're a creative thinker, come up with an original way to describe what you do.

WHAT TO INCLUDE

As usual, it's not the trait or skill itself that is useful to an employer; it's putting your creativity into practice to benefit the business. So make sure your examples show that benefit clearly.

If you don't think you're creative, or can't think of any examples, try thinking along these lines. There may well be some crossover with using your initiative. Have you ever wondered why something at work is done the way it is? Could it be improved? If so, your ideas or how you changed something for the better could be a great example of creativity:

▶ devising a new process to save time or money
▶ bringing together an unexpected group of people to solve a problem
▶ doing the opposite of what competitors are doing, increasing your market share
▶ reading something very different in a new trend or piece of research, which leads to a new direction that becomes very profitable
▶ seeing a link between sales performance and, say, the weather to make marketing more effective.

Insight
The more limited the situation, often the more creative the solution. If you've solved a tough problem, you have probably shown creativity, so it's worth giving an example. The problem could be anything from how to deliver the same quality on a smaller budget, to how to get people's support for something you're working on.

Example

'Our team manages lots of time-sensitive projects for customers. Key people often seemed to be away when needed most, and no one remembered that they'd be on holiday. Personnel captured all holidays on a shared database, but no one managed to check it regularly when busy. So I suggested adding a footer to everyone's email, to show their next "out of office" date(s) in red.

'Now, as critical dates approach on a given project, we are all much more aware of any absences and can plan around them.

Customers are also more aware of when their main contact will be away, which really helps, too. It took moments to implement and takes moments to update. It has improved our contingency planning, we waste less time, and our customers are happier with response times. We've grown our business by 20 per cent since then, and with none of the chaos we feared.'

It doesn't have to be ground-breaking stuff, just a new way of doing things. Even if you're 16 and have been working as a shelf stacker in the supermarket, you can still show creativity in your job:

'I noticed the store was very busy at certain times, which also seemed to be when we had big stock cages out in each aisle for restocking shelves. It was causing blockages in the aisles that often hampered customers.

'Rather than waiting until a product started to run out, I suggested that we bring the cages out earlier in the day and aim for full shelves just before the busiest period. This saved time, because there were fewer disruptions while we filled the shelves, and it meant that the cages were in the storeroom for the busiest times.

'Customers got round the store quicker and happier; and possibly because we were then able to spend more time helping customers, they started spending more.'

Question 37: Thinking back over your career/ last job, what sort of risks did you take? Did they pay off?

WHY IS IT ASKED?

Not all businesses or roles require a person who likes to take big risks. In fact, relatively few do. However, it is often through taking risks – be it in the form a radical product, a different approach, a new partnership, a change of image, a bold statement – that companies make major advances.

So, risk taking is likely to be part of any role you want to make a success of. If you're always playing it safe, never taking any risks, then your job is likely to plod along rather than go stellar.

COMMON MISTAKES

Thinking the interviewer is looking for someone who shares characteristics with Nick Leeson, the trader whose decision to take a virtually unlimited risk had the power to make millions or bring the company crashing down.

WHAT TO INCLUDE

Employers appreciate someone who can assess a situation, look at different options, and make a decision to take a calculated, limited risk to get a worthwhile benefit.

If you're not quite sure what constitutes taking a risk, it could be anything that involves a trade-off:

▶ Being more assertive with a customer risks losing their custom, but the upside might be a much bigger order. Is the reward worth the risk?

▶ Taking on extra responsibility could improve your chances of promotion, but you risk overstretching yourself and letting something else slide. Is this reward worth the risk?

Example

'I suggested we offer a trolley dash as a prize in a local event. The upside would be extra interest in our store, more people shopping on event day, maybe some new customers, and good PR in the community. The risk was that there might be no uplift in sales: we could give away hundreds of pounds' worth of groceries for nothing.

'I considered managing this risk by limiting the value of the trolley dash: keeping it to one minute instead of two, or saying that alcohol was excluded. I toyed with the idea of offering £400 in vouchers – but that would create less excitement.

'So I decided to take the risk and offer the more exciting trolley dash, with all the added publicity that would entail. I did specify no alcohol, to limit the risk, and it was a huge success. Our sales increased by 22 per cent that day, and by an average of 4 per cent over the following two months.'

'We reached a critical point in the company's development when, to expand, we needed higher turnover.

'I wanted the sales team to approach bigger customers and get them on board, but the risk was that we wouldn't be able to deliver what we promised if the growth happened too rapidly. If we let a new customer down once, we'd likely be unable to win them back. We could target less valuable medium-sized customers, but the most important factor was rapid growth.

'So I decided to take the risk and approach the bigger customers we'd always wanted. We kept the manufacturing team well informed – if they knew when demand peaks and troughs would come, they could plan better for it. And it did pay off: our turnover has grown by almost 30 per cent this last year, and so far that's without letting any customers down.'

13

....

Tougher or more searching questions

In this chapter you will learn:
- *how to respond positively to tough, often negatively phrased questions.*

You may view these questions with suspicion or fear, but what makes a question more searching, challenging or tough often has little to do with the content and everything to do with the phrasing. You'll see the same fundamental topics are coming up again and again, just wearing different clothes.

Question 38: How do you handle change when you don't agree with it?

WHY IS IT ASKED?

This is a clever question. It is asking you about your reactions to one of the most awkward and yet common situations at work.

Every business must change to survive, especially in difficult economic times, and some have to adapt very rapidly to create an advantage over the competition. Yet, at heart, most people are resistant to change, although there's often a distinct divide between management and the rest of the employees.

Managing a team, department or organization successfully is achieved by inspiring good performance and meeting objectives, which often involves trying to do something differently. So managers will normally, by definition, spend a significant portion of their time bringing about change.

The rest of the workforce often spends its time resisting change because people don't understand it, or because it affects the role they were comfortable doing every day.

COMMON MISTAKES

Giving the impression you might be resistant to change. Employees who are, especially if they are vocal about it, can be damaging to morale and to the organization's performance as a whole.

Being a 'yes man'. There's no shame in appropriately questioning or challenging change (up to a point) and simply agreeing with everything you're told doesn't allow you to add real value.

WHAT TO INCLUDE

Employers want people who are adaptable and who can see the point of change and support it; whose priority is to help the company meet its objectives, not their own personal preferences.

An employee who questions change and seeks to understand it will be more desirable to most than someone who resists it, or doesn't care.

Example

'I'm pretty adaptable when it comes to change, although if given a choice I'd always ask how any changes in my role or team relate to the wider company. Once I understand change, I can really get behind it.

'Our department was recently sent a memo asking us to update every product planogram on our system by the end of the month. This was a huge amount of work and a very tight deadline; several team members were unhappy. I asked my manager to explain further and he said annual terms negotiations, starting the following month, were being radically overhauled.

'Once my team understood that the entire sales force was relying on us and that the deadline wasn't set on a whim, the atmosphere changed – all of us took real pride in making sure we hit that deadline.'

Question 39: What's the worst thing about your current employer?

WHY IS IT ASKED?

This is a roundabout way of finding out why you're leaving; and working out whether your reason for going would give you potential problems in your new job. It's cleverly phrased so that you feel obliged to raise a negative point.

COMMON MISTAKES

Getting caught out by the negative phrasing and slating a former employer. So what if your boss is a burned-out 'Type A' personality who physically twitches from the stress he is under and has taken to barking in his office; or if she undermines all your efforts and has taken to correcting your typos with a red pen? Most of us have struggled to get along with a boss at some point; it's one of the most common reasons we start to look around for something else. But in this case, knowing what the worst thing is doesn't mean you should say it aloud.

Insight

Don't try to dodge the question by say something like: 'Oh, but I love everything about my current employer.' You are at this interview with a view to leaving your current employer, so the cynic would argue that there must be something you're missing. Claiming everything is perfect can seem insincere.

WHAT TO INCLUDE

Go for the middle ground. There are two routes you could take:

1 Try to find something relatively innocuous about the company you work for and claim that this is the worst thing; the implication will be that everything else is just dandy.
2 Start with lots of positives, then include a less positive aspect that most people could identify with.

Be consistent: make sure that anything you say here agrees with previous questions you've answered about your ideal/worst boss, why you want to join this company, etc.

'Probably the food! The canteen is geared towards the shift workers and serves rich, heavy meals. But it doesn't really bother me; I just take a packed lunch instead.'

Or:

'The new expense system – it takes forever to create the simplest claim and everyone loses hours on it. We've all given feedback to the development team, but it's just a bit of a niggle while we wait for the next stage.'

'There's not much not to like, to be honest – I've got a great boss who delegates lots of responsibility to her team, so I get plenty of challenges and yet feel really well supported. If I had to name something to improve, it would probably be the development and training opportunities. I love my job but feel it's time to build on my leadership skills, which is why I'm so keen on this role with your organization.'

Question 40: You say you have a sense of humour – prove it. Make me laugh. Tell me a joke.

WHY IS IT ASKED?

Partly to put you on the spot; and quite possibly to also draw out some kind of proof that you do have a sense of humour.

COMMON MISTAKES

Thinking you have to tell a joke. You may feel you will lose points by not saying something funny, or perhaps you have an absolute cracker on the tip of your tongue; but telling a joke can be a huge mistake.

However great the joke, however fantastic your sense of humour, however carefully you've selected one that cannot possibly be construed as racist, feminist, misogynist, ageist or otherwise discriminatory, what if the interviewer *doesn't* share your sense of humour? What if you tell your joke and it meets with a blank stare, a pitying smile, or outrage?

WHAT TO INCLUDE

Not a joke. You're likely to be far better off talking your way out of this one politely but firmly.

'I'm quick to see the funny side of things and to have a laugh at work, without being unprofessional. Colleagues tell me that my perspective often makes them smile or helps a stressful day pass more easily. But what I can't claim to be is a comedian. Even if I could bring to mind a good joke right now, I'm not sure it would be an asset to my interview!'

Question 41: What is your work/life balance? Have you got it about right?

WHY IS IT ASKED?

This is a curious question. In practice, most employers probably wouldn't turn down a workaholic, provided they're pleasant to work with and don't show signs of burning out. However, being a rounded person is considered quite important by some organizations, and it's true that people tend to perform better if they get a chance to play as well as work.

COMMON MISTAKES

Saying you don't have time for a life outside work. This might suggest you are on your way to burning out.

Enthusing about your extracurricular activities to such a degree that your participation might negatively affect your performance at work, or make you inflexible when it comes to overtime, travel, or anything else job-related.

Insight

Beware of mentioning high-risk hobbies without thought. Yes, they are memorable, but if the risk of injury is high then they might not be so appealing. Few employers relish the prospect of managing cover for long-term absences while key personnel recover from their base-jumping injuries.

WHAT TO INCLUDE

As is so often the case, a balanced answer is likely to be best. Ideal is having activities and interests outside work that you enjoy and have enough time to pursue, some of which may even help you develop additional skills useful to your work.

Whether you think you have it about right or you don't, it doesn't necessarily matter; what's often more important is that you are *aware* of needing to have a work/life balance, of its importance to your well-being, and that you can and will take steps to put it right if the balance gets upset.

This question also gives you a chance to talk about activities outside work that may show another side of you, imply further useful skills, and help the interviewer to get a sense of your character as a potential colleague rather than a candidate on paper. Your hobbies may also make you more memorable, which can be to your advantage.

Example

'I think my work/life balance is pretty good. I do work long hours, but it's a very satisfying role, and it still leaves me enough time to spend at home and to indulge my hobbies on the weekends. Flying is my real passion: neither lessons nor aircraft come cheap, so that's another motivating factor for me to sell hard. And the great thing is, with a PPL you can fly from almost any airfield, so my flying can coexist with my career, wherever it may lead.'

Question 42: Have you ever been involved in a legal wrangle with an employer?

WHY IS IT ASKED?

Most employers, regardless of the background, reasons or fairness of the situation, take a dim view of anyone who has engaged in a legal battle with their employer. However unfairly, engaging in legal action suggests a combative type of person who may not be afraid to cause trouble in their organization should something not suit them. It matters little what actually happened – just that it did.

COMMON MISTAKES

Lying about a tribunal or court case. This is not advisable as you may be asked the question *because* they've done their research and are keen to hear your side of the story. If you lie, you'll likely ruin your chances of anything else you say being taken seriously.

WHAT TO INCLUDE

If you haven't, it's a one word answer – 'No.' If this is a situation you have been in, your best bet is to prepare a brief, positive story about what happened and why the legal action arose, what you learned from the process, and what you will do differently in future should similar circumstances arise. If you somehow remained with the same employer afterwards, and there appear to be no hard feelings on either side, that would be very much worth mentioning.

Example

'I would normally be extremely reluctant to take my employer to court, but unfortunately I lost my job for something I hadn't done, and it took a court case to get back my good name and the job I loved. I don't regret going through it, as I stayed in my job for a further two years before moving into the more senior position I'm in now, but it was certainly regrettable.'

If asked for more detail about what happened:

'I was suspended then fired for gross misconduct, allegedly for harassing a male colleague via email. I completely understood the company's zero tolerance of harassment, but it wasn't me that had sent the incriminating emails. Detailed investigation proved that a colleague had used my PC while I was away from my desk; when questioned, the individual confessed it had been meant as a joke but he had felt too scared to own up once it escalated. I have no problem with the disciplinary action my employer took, given the company's policies on discrimination, and it's reassuring to know that if I was ever a victim there would be a support system in place. It's just a pity things had reached the courts before the truth was established. Now, I have an excellent security system that locks my computer down when I leave my desk, so I won't suffer the consequences of a similar prank again.'

Question 43: What do you think of the news about [today's headline]?

WHY IS IT ASKED?

Who wouldn't prefer a workforce made up of informed people with a healthy interest in society and the world around them? A regular paper reader (even if it's only once a week) is more likely to pick up some knowledge about a lot of different things that could enhance their perspective on a work issue, add to their creativity or just give them something interesting to talk about.

> **Insight**
> Even if you have little time for current affairs, seriously consider starting to read a paper (even if you drop it later) if you're job hunting. At the least, try to read a newspaper (or listen to/watch the news) in the days before, and on the morning of, your interview.

COMMON MISTAKES

Being too extreme. If asked your opinion of a specific headline, or a news item you mentioned, be cautious how strongly you state your case. Most businesses benefit from people who can appraise a situation objectively and weigh up evidence before making a judgement or decision. The thinking also goes that people who display strong emotional responses to an event, or hold extreme opinions about certain subjects, may lack objectivity at work and be less effective.

Trying to bluff your way through a headline/story you haven't even heard of and know nothing about. Be honest: say you're not aware of this news item and could they outline it to you briefly?

WHAT TO INCLUDE

It's worth showing with your answer that you've assessed both sides of the story and can appreciate the news item from more than one viewpoint. You may get questioned on this in more detail, or asked to justify your opinion, so be well prepared.

'I was reading about last night's explosion at the Hinkley Point nuclear reactor. I'm fascinated by the safety systems nuclear reactors have; the way they have so much redundancy built in, with back-ups to handle almost every contingency. Hopefully the explosion is something that these systems can easily handle. But if I lived nearby, I still think I'd be concerned: after all, there aren't many steps between a nuclear "incident" and a Chernobyl-scale disaster.'

Then...

'Am I a fan of nuclear power? That's an interesting question. I think, like any energy source, it has its drawbacks – particularly safety concerns over the handling of the nuclear fuel before, during and after use – but I can also see there are financial and environmental arguments for relying on nuclear power more heavily in future. Despite my concerns I do accept that, based on current alternatives, there appears to be a genuine need for the new wave of nuclear power stations currently being built.'

Question 44: How much do you earn in your current role?

Interviewers may say it's because they want to see if candidates can assess their true value – but most of the time they just want to know how much they'll likely need to offer you if they want to hire you.

COMMON MISTAKES

Lying about, or exaggerating, your current salary. Your current employer is likely to be asked this as part of your reference, so there is a very good chance you'll be found out.

WHAT TO INCLUDE

There is a strongly held belief among most job hunters – perhaps wishful thinking – that your next employer will match or exceed your current salary. So by telling them a higher salary, you increase your chances of getting more money the next time around. This may often be true, but how much do you puff your salary up by? You could price yourself out of a job offer and get written off because the company thinks it can't afford you or you're being unrealistic and overvaluing yourself.

If your current salary is high, relative to the marketplace, just mention your salary and leave it at that. There's plenty of time to discuss the finer points or the whole package when you get to offer stage.

If your current salary is low compared to the marketplace, there may be a natural tendency to want to puff up your current earnings, especially if your income is a lot lower than the income bracket of the job you are applying for. Understandably you don't want to appear devalued or out of your depth. The most effective answer is to state your salary package, rather than just your salary. Only justify it if you feel you can do so positively.

Example – low salary

'I currently earn £14,500 a year plus a company Audi, private health cover and a non-contributory pension.'

Or mention other positive aspects of your remuneration:

'My salary is £14,500 a year, the very top bracket for my level at Sharps & Son. Since the salary freeze two years ago, I've been rewarded for my excellent performance in other ways: funding for my season ticket, annual gym membership, and additional accredited training courses of my choosing, which brings my package to around £19,500.'

Or:

'I'm on £14,500 a year. I recognize this is at the lower end for the industry, but I've been happy with this until now because the training is second to none and I've saved over £5,500 a year by being able to walk to work instead of buying a season ticket to London.'

'£37,500 per year.'

If you are concerned the interviewer may think you're blagging because it's so high, you could briefly mention the responsibilities or skills that enable you to command this:

'£37,500 per year. It's not industry typical for a sales forecaster, but my financial background meant I took on responsibility for increasing the profitability of the seasonal ranges, so my salary reflects the additional value I bring to the role.'

Question 45: We have been in touch with one of your referees and, although their feedback was generally positive, there was one area they expressed concern about. I'm curious to see if you know what it might have been?

Other variants could include:

▶ 'One of our staff here says they've worked with you before and that you tended to pursue your goals single-mindedly, no matter what the risks. Is that true?'
▶ 'What's the most unfair thing you've ever had said or written about you at work?'

WHY IS IT ASKED?

This is just another way of asking about your performance in the eyes of others. Obviously, if you didn't supply references with your CV, then it's not a question you'll need to worry about.

This could be a blatant attempt to catch you out. It's possible they haven't contacted your referees and are just testing you – but whether the question is genuine or not, your answer should be the same. If they want to ask you about your weaknesses, they can do so openly: don't hand them anything on a plate.

COMMON MISTAKES

Simply listing all your shortcomings, one after the other, until the interviewer nods.

WHAT TO INCLUDE

The best approach is to appear surprised at the question, and to justify your surprise by saying that you've had positive feedback in all the areas mentioned as relevant to this job.

In case this *is* a genuine question, try then admitting that you'd love to know what it was your referee said about you, as you appreciate all feedback. If it's a bluff, the interviewer will either admit it or not, before moving on. If it's real, then it's a good idea to raise this issue because it means you can deal with it now.

Hopefully, genuine feedback will never be a complete surprise but there's nothing wrong with disputing your referee's concerns if you can give some examples to support your argument. Don't let this feedback be swept aside in the hope that the interviewer will forget about it: use it to change the interviewer's perception of you.

Example

'That comes as a surprise – I'm really not sure what it could have been, as the feedback I had in my last appraisal was great. My boss gave me a positive rating for my all-round communication and presentation skills, for getting along with the whole team, and for my proactive problem-solving and analytical ability. May I ask what the concern was raised about?'

Interviewer response: 'It was about your public speaking ability.'

'That's strange. I did a public speaking course in my previous job and as well as using it for internal training, I have been asked to give a talk at our industry conference for the past three years. So I'm a little confused why a concern about my public speaking would have been raised, unless there was perhaps a misunderstanding?'

Question 46: If we were to give you a firm job offer...

- ▶ '...would you accept?'
- ▶ '...how much would we need to pay you?'
- ▶ '...when could you start?'
- ▶ '...how would you feel?'
- ▶ '...would you resign tomorrow?'

WHY IS IT ASKED?

This question could be pitched any number of ways but the thing to note is that it is a HYPOTHETICAL question: *if* we were to offer you a job. The interviewer is trying to gauge how much you want the job and what they'd have to do to get you.

COMMON MISTAKES

This is NOT a job offer, so don't get too carried away with your answer as if it is.

WHAT TO INCLUDE

'...would you accept?'

The best way to answer this kind of question is to show genuine enthusiasm: this is what you really want. However, don't give everything away and say you'd accept, before knowing exactly what it is you'd be accepting.

Example

'I'd be really delighted – I am very keen on this role – and I would ask to hear the details of your offer.'

'...how much would we need to pay you?'

No employer wants to pay more than they have to for the employee they want. Many will try to work out where to pitch their starting point for any negotiation that may follow. If they're able to go as high as £50k and you say they'd need to pay you £33k, they're laughing if you turn out to be the person they want. Conversely, if they're prepared to pay £33k and you demand £50k, they may think twice about making you an offer that's likely to be rejected. It's a real dilemma in any interview.

If you wish to try and avoid answering and feel bold enough, you could try reversing the question.

Example

'Well, I'd want to first understand the exact hours, responsibilities, and overall package that the offer would involve, then I could give you an appropriate salary range.'

Otherwise your best bet would be to mention an appropriate range of salaries, dependent on the exact nature of the job and any other benefits.

Example

'It would really depend on the offer details and the opportunities for further training and progression within the company; but as a guide I'd be looking for something in the £25–30k range.'

'…when could you start?'

You should be aware what your notice period is and whether any unused holiday could reduce that. The job advert may say they want someone to start as soon as possible, or the start date could be two months from now, or it may not mention start dates at all. The interviewer may mention an ideal date, but may not.

If you're not aware of any time constraint, then it's up to you what potential start date you give. If you would like a short break before starting your new role, keep this in mind – but remember that earlier availability is often more attractive.

Insight

If time is of the essence and you really do want this job, it might not be good to build in extra weeks so you can take a break. Quote your standard notice period at interview and then, once they want you and have put an offer on the table, you could try to negotiate a later start date. They may not agree, but at least you'd be arguing from a stronger position.

Example

'My notice period is one month: if I accepted a firm offer, I'd be happy to resign immediately.'

Question 47: Other candidates have achieved much more than you in a similar amount of time at school/university or since graduating/leaving school. Where have you fallen short, or not made as much of opportunities as you could have?

WHY IS IT ASKED?

It's a negatively phrased question designed to get you to admit you haven't done so well in certain areas. It's a pressure tactic, one designed to weed out people who haven't prepared well or who allow their nerves to overcome them in a stressful situation.

COMMON MISTAKES

Falling into the trap of agreeing you haven't done as well as you should or have missed opportunities, just because the interviewer asks a negatively framed question.

WHAT TO INCLUDE

Interpret this question more positively and answer this instead: how have you made the most of your time during/since your education? What opportunities have you taken? What have you learned? How have you developed or progressed? Why are you satisfied with/proud of where you are at this point in your education/career?

With a positive approach, you can fend off questions like this and remind the interviewer of your strong points.

Example – leaving education

'Actually, I'm quite pleased with where I am.

'I've studied hard throughout school and college, and got good results in my academic work, particularly Maths, English and Business Studies, which are most relevant to this role and the career path I want to take.

'I held down a part-time job throughout my course, so I've also gained experience working in a team, dealing with the public, and

I've proved I can think on my feet even under pressure. I also played hard, as part of the college football team – I was captain in my final year, and we reached the semi-final of a national tournament.

So I feel I've really made the most of every opportunity that has come my way – and I'm hoping to continue doing so in this role.'

'I can't speak for any other candidates, but I'm very pleased with my current situation.

'My commitment to study paid off at school, and my exam results helped me to land a great first job with Brilliance UK. I brought the same level of commitment to that role, and before long was the youngest person to be promoted.

'I requested additional training in advanced communication and facilitation, and a year later I spotted the perfect opening for a supervisor at United Stars. Within a year there, I'd applied for a team leader role. Despite great feedback, they felt my experience was not yet broad enough so I then negotiated a six-month secondment in a different department, after which I got the team leader position I'd wanted.

'I've been doing that role successfully for the past two years and am now ready for my next challenge. I feel really happy with my rapid progress so far, much of which I put down to the opportunities I've created for myself.'

Question 48: If I called your company right now and asked to speak to you urgently, where would they say you were?

WHY IS IT ASKED?

This seems like an odd question, but the interviewer may just want to know whether you have been open, circumspect or untruthful about your interview today. They sometimes just want to see your initial reaction to the question, so if you're expecting it then it shouldn't catch you out.

COMMON MISTAKES

Saying they'd say you were off sick. Lying is usually frowned upon by employers, and pulling a sickie to go for a job interview doesn't make you seem like the most loyal or dedicated employee.

WHAT TO INCLUDE

Your boss may know exactly where you are and may support you in your job search. But if the vacancy you are being interviewed for is being filled on a confidential basis – and you work for a competitor – it may be better not to say your boss knows exactly where you are, only that they know you are attending an interview.

If your employer has no idea you are job hunting, that's also fine. Most people keep their activities quiet until they have a firm offer. But taking a day or half-day's annual leave would be looked upon better than taking a sick day.

Example

'I imagine they'd simply say I was on leave and back tomorrow. They don't know where I am at the moment, only that I booked a day's holiday.'

Question 49: For you, what's the biggest downside to working here?

WHY IS IT ASKED?

Another negatively phrased question to catch you out if you are less keen on the role or company than you appear to be.

COMMON MISTAKES

Instantly coming up with something negative about working there. It will make you seem less keen on the job. The next question could be: 'Doesn't that put you off, then?'

WHAT TO INCLUDE

Unless you can think of a trivial downside, or a short-term downside that will disappear quickly (such as the temporary hassle of relocating) and is outweighed by all the upsides, then it is worth saying you can't see any downsides to working here.

If you have done your research properly and know a little about the company, you may find it easier to come up with something minor, provided you offset it with all the positive aspects you've identified about working there.

Insight

If you *can* see a big downside, or discover one during the interview, it's still best not to mention it directly. Afterwards, think carefully about whether it's something you can live with: if you don't think you can, then you can always turn down the offer if they make one.

Example

'I don't feel there is a downside for me, which is partly why I'm so attracted to this role. I'll be working with an enthusiastic team and great products. I know my experience will add lots of value and I can bring lots of ideas for improving efficiency. And from what you've described, there are fantastic opportunities for training and progression, which is really important to me.

'If I had to pick something, it would be that your offices are near a rugby stadium rather than a football stadium, so I'll have to go a little further afield to catch a game after work – but that's minor as I'd far rather be in the right job, whatever the location.'

Question 50: Why has it been/was it so hard for you to find a new job when you were made redundant/left your last job?

WHY IS IT ASKED?

It's asked because it's negatively phrased, which makes it tougher to handle. They could have asked 'What happened here, then?' or 'What did you do after you were made redundant?', but this plays on the implicit suggestion that if there's a big gap in your career history, you must have found it hard to get someone to employ you. There must therefore be something wrong with you.

COMMON MISTAKES

Flinching if you're asked this question. If you've already prepared and practised the most upbeat story you can, the dread won't show on your face and your answer will come across positively.

WHAT TO INCLUDE

Handling any gap-related questions is best done by focusing on the positives you gained from time out of paid work. These positives could include almost anything:

▶ training or studying that built upon your skills or knowledge
▶ satisfying volunteer work that built upon your skills
▶ highly selective job research/search that led to a great opportunity
▶ retraining, or re-evaluating your career
▶ personal or cultural enrichment, travel or teaching abroad
▶ freelance or consulting opportunities
▶ caring for a dependant or raising a young family for a time
▶ the chance to recover your health fully or return to full capability
▶ renovating a house, car or other personal project now complete.

If you took some time to get back into paid work, it may be because you had something else that you wanted or needed to do, learn or try, or that you were being very selective about the kind of role you wanted to get. There's nothing wrong with saying that, as long as you are happy with your answer so it comes across as genuine. If you feel awkward or guilty about the gap, it could look as if you are lying about something.

If you don't feel very comfortable answering this question, you'll need to rehearse – maybe a lot – until you truly believe that being out of work was a positive experience and can say so with confidence. Then it's much easier to convince someone else.

'I was made redundant at quite short notice and there were no positions advertised at the time that would really progress my career, so I decided to wait for the right one.

'I knew that to get a more management-oriented position I'd need more leadership experience, so I did a training course in inspirational management and strategic team planning. I put this into practice by volunteering for three months as event co-ordinator for a local hospice. My new skills helped me pull together a mix of staff and volunteers, with very diverse abilities and motivations, into one of the most successful fundraising teams the hospice ever had.

'Shortly after, I found the kind of role I'd been waiting for. My leadership skills gave me the edge over other candidates so I was very glad to have had the opportunity to develop them sooner than I'd otherwise have done.'

'I was made redundant about three months ago and I've viewed it as a great chance to spend time looking into the R&D functions of a broad range of companies to identify my next step. I've made a shortlist of five blue-chip companies that would really benefit from my skills, and where there are significant opportunities to broaden my experience and progress.

All the companies are in very different industries but have the same reliance on new product development, a large R&D department and a strong record of innovation. Your company is one of them, so I'm really excited about the opportunity you're currently advertising and I'm hoping my being so selective will pay off.'

Question 51: Are you prepared to put yourself 'out there'?

WHY IS IT ASKED?

The interviewer has a specific trait or set of traits in mind that they feel will be positive for this role. The challenge of this type of question is understanding exactly what they mean by it, and in thinking up an example on the spot.

COMMON MISTAKES

Saying yes under pressure, when you don't know exactly what it means. This could back you into a corner if you're then asked to give an example of how you've put yourself 'out there' in the past? It's quite acceptable to ask the interviewer to explain what they mean by 'out there'. Saying no, as the main reason this would be asked is to establish if you have something they want.

WHAT TO INCLUDE

If the interviewer clarifies 'out there' like this – 'Well, would you be prepared to dye your own hair or give yourself a skin treatment in store, for example, to demonstrate our products to a customer?' – then the question is not difficult.

It's a closed question, so a yes or no answer is acceptable, but try to be a little more enthusiastic. If you can think up an example as proof of when you've put yourself 'out there' in the past, that's even better.

Example

'Absolutely! I change my hair colour every couple of months anyway, so I'd really enjoy it, and I love using your skin products. I'm not too shy to get stuck into something like this in front of other people: a few weeks ago I modelled a mini dress made out of newspaper in front of 400 people for our school's trash fashion show, and I loved it!'

Question 52: What will you do if you don't get this job?

WHY IS IT ASKED?

This is another hypothetical question and a pressure tactic, to see how you react when (presumably) disappointed.

COMMON MISTAKES

To overreact or overstate your case. 'Kill myself' is not the answer they are hoping for – they don't need staff who are that dedicated or that unstable. Not to show anything at all. The interviewer might think you don't really care whether or not you get the job, rather than admiring your lack of emotion.

WHAT TO INCLUDE

You need to communicate how deeply disappointing this would be (you'd give anything to get this job, right?) while showing how pragmatic you can be when it comes to disappointment. You can also drop in again how much you want the job and how good at it you'd be.

Example

'Inside I'd be gutted. I've spent so long researching this organization and this role, and I'd really love to work here. But rather than dwell on the negatives, I think I'd firstly ask you why you weren't going to offer me this job, and then see if there was any way I could address your concerns during the remainder of the interview.

'If I wasn't able to address your concerns in full, then I'd ask if you knew of any other opportunities within the company or vacancies that might arise soon, in case there was another entry route I hadn't considered.

'If there were, I'd ask if any application I made would be welcome and considered, and, if not, what I might be able to do to improve my chances.'

Question 53: Which person, from any period in your working history, would you least like to work with again, and why?

WHY IS IT ASKED?

To cleverly draw out of you the kind of person you've had problems with in the past. This can illuminate things like your working style, or how you like to be managed.

Instantly naming someone without apparent thought – it makes it look as if working with them was really terrible for you to endure.

Casting aspersions on their character, ability or working style. This will suggest that you can't work successfully with people who are challenging or awkward in any way.

WHAT TO INCLUDE

Time for apparent reflection, even if you know what you're going to say. Think of someone who was difficult to work with for reasons that do not reflect on you, so that it's about them and not you.

Bring your answer around to the positives of working with this particular person, so that it isn't a negatively phrased answer that looks as if you are the complaining type.

Example

'That's a tough one – I've got along really well with everyone I've worked with. I can't think of anyone I wouldn't happily work with again. Hmm… if pushed I'd probably have to say one of the commodities buyers in my first job: he was so bright, really stimulating to work with, but he suffered from terrible breath – which did make it a little testing to work physically closely with him on projects. Fortunately he spent a lot of time travelling so much of our work was conducted by phone and email, so I was able to focus on his ideas rather than his last meal.'

14

Job-specific questions

In this chapter you will learn about:
- *job-specific questions and how to respond to them effectively.*

Depending on the role you are applying for, job-specific questions could be about almost anything. The only guidelines for answering these are that you should be sure you understand the question, and are honest and succinct with your response.

A good way to protect yourself is to ensure that you definitely do have any skills, knowledge and experience that you claim to on your CV. Research any job-specific skills, experience or knowledge mentioned in the job advert that you may be weak on.

Potential questions

The list is endless, depending on the role and your background, but you may be asked something along these lines:

- ▶ 'What experiences have you had implementing the ISO 9001 Quality Management System?'
- ▶ 'Would you use Javascript or PHP to create a fully dynamic website? Why?'
- ▶ 'Why would you be interested in doing legal aid work? If you wouldn't, why not?'
- ▶ 'Where do you stand on equal opportunities? Have you introduced any policies to support this?'
- ▶ 'How many people have you successfully placed in this industry?'

- ▶ 'Can you spot the mistake in these 50 lines of text/programming/ calculations?'
- ▶ 'You claim to be numerate. Without using a calculator, please add these 20 numbers.'
- ▶ 'If you were designing a pyramid-shaped box that shouldn't require gluing, what would be wrong with this CAD layout?'

Answering

Sample answers for job-specific questions are impossible, but some guidelines may help:

- ▶ If you don't understand something, ask for it to be clarified.
- ▶ If you need a piece of paper for your workings, ask upfront.
- ▶ State your answer, as simply and briefly as you can.
- ▶ If it requires justification or explanation of your reasoning or workings, try to do this in less than a minute.
- ▶ Try to relate your answer back to how well qualified you are for the role.

15

'What if' questions

In this chapter you will learn:
- *how to cope with hypothetical questions.*

Some people consider these very tricky, because it's not always obvious what the interviewer is looking for.

'What if' questions normally relate to characteristics, skills or experience mentioned in the job advert. So, as with any interview answer, aim to mention the relevant qualities, skills or experience they are asking for. Try to give an example of what you've done in the past to help explain why you would choose that course of action.

You cannot prepare fully for questions like this. Sometimes you'll be asked about a situation you've been in before, or something very similar, so when answering you can give an example of how you've successfully used this approach, solution or skill before. Sometimes the 'What if' will take you somewhere you've never been. All you can do is be clear in your mind about the kind of skills and qualities they're looking for, then give the best answer you can.

Popular topics

The most commonly used topics relate to parts of the job advert or job description, although 'What if?' questions are also used to get into other, more generally desirable traits such as integrity or honesty. Topics may include the following:

▶ management issues, such as handling awkward disciplinary proceedings
▶ legal issues relating to your job or industry

- ▶ job-specific issues, such as dealing with an abusive customer
- ▶ company/organizational policy
- ▶ integrity
- ▶ coping with change or disappointment
- ▶ giving up something for work, for example being in a band.

Potential question areas are discussed in this chapter, but specific questions and example answers are generally not given other than to illustrate key points, because hypothetical answers always have so many variables.

Management issues

For a managerial role, you might be asked questions about how you would deal with an awkward situation. This might include:

- ▶ handling a serious grievance, such as discrimination
- ▶ firing someone
- ▶ dealing with an employee who cries during a disciplinary meeting
- ▶ having to make half your team redundant
- ▶ resolving conflict between team members
- ▶ motivating an underperformer.

Go through in your mind how you would handle situations like these, especially if management responsibility is or will be part of your job. It may also help if you do some research into the company's policies in these areas, so you can see the kind of approach they like to take as an organization. Finally, check the advert again to remind yourself which qualities they seek in employees; use these criteria to inform your answer.

Legal issues

Not just for would-be lawyers. Being aware of relevant laws can be useful in any number of other roles. And whatever the role, the more senior it is the more likely it will include some management responsibility – for which it may help if you have some understanding of employment law.

You might need to be aware of: food hygiene legislation if you're in catering; planning or building legislation if you're a developer, architect or surveyor; financial legislation if you're a trader in an investment bank; housing legislation if you work for a housing association, or consumer legislation if you're in retail.

Even if you are not directly responsible for applying legislation to your daily work, it never hurts to be aware that it exists and has an impact on your employer.

Job-specific issues

Depending on your role, you could be quizzed on almost anything:

▶ As a teacher or teaching assistant, you might be asked how you would accommodate a special needs child in a given situation, or what you'd do if you suspected a child in your class of being abused.

▶ Police recruits could be asked about any number of situations, such as how you'd defuse a volatile situation in a crowded pub, what you'd do if someone's life was in grave danger but you had no back-up, or how you'd handle a large group of youths on a housing estate being threatening to other residents.

▶ A call centre operative might be asked how they would handle a difficult or abusive caller.

The best way to prepare for this kind of question is to understand in as much depth as possible what the job will entail, as well as the qualities and skills the employer wants in a new recruit. That means research – which you will hopefully have already done. Whether it's your first job or a next step in your career, there's no excuse for not knowing what you'll be doing in the job you're applying for. You might find a lot of similarities with the job you're doing now, in which case you could be asked about familiar challenges or situations.

FAMILIAR SITUATIONS

A customer service call centre wants people with good telephone communication skills, who stay calm under pressure, are always polite and represent the company in a professional manner. Think about how you could use your answers to show that you have these qualities and remember to include proof from your past experience, if you can.

'What would you do if you answered a call and the customer was ranting, saying, "What rubbish service!" – because they've been on hold for ten minutes?'

Remember they're looking for calm, polite and professional people in the advert.

'Well, I'd *calmly* apologize for any delay in getting through, and then ask what I could do to help them. And then I'd let them talk. In my last customer service job, I learned that trying to justify a problem by saying something like "I'm sorry, we're unusually busy today" often doesn't help. If anything, it seems to make some people worse because then they start to attack the reason you've given. I find that apologizing *politely* and asking how I can help, in a *professional* manner, tends to bring most customers back to their normal, more polite way of talking.'

UNFAMILIAR SITUATIONS

Other times you may be given a situation you've never faced before. You can try practising answers to this type of question, if it helps them seem less daunting – you can often find useful information or likely questions from looking online – but you will still have to think on your feet, no matter how much preparation you do.

If you can justify your answer based on a related personal experience, it will add weight.

Company/organizational policy

Use your research to be as up to date as possible on the organization's policies. Depending on the job you're going for, it might be policies about anything from health and safety or equal opportunities to environmental policy, confidentiality or treating service users with respect.

If you've done your research then if you are asked a related 'What if?' question, you will know how the organization would normally prefer to handle the matter.

Integrity

You could be asked almost anything to 'test' personal qualities such as integrity, honesty, perseverance or determination. Integrity questions might tackle what you'd do if you spotted a colleague's minor misdemeanour, or if you witnessed gross misconduct such as theft, bullying or harassment. It could also be to do with how you would own up to, or correct, a mistake internally. Questions may be of the type 'What would you do if...?':

▶ '...you saw a colleague with their hand in the till?'
▶ '...you saw a colleague writing down customers' credit card details?'
▶ '...you overheard someone making a sexist remark to a colleague?'
▶ '...you were in a big meeting and you spotted your boss had made a mistake with their figures?'
▶ '...someone presented your colleague's idea to management, passing it off as their own?'

You need to consider the needs of your employer when thinking about your answer, although most matters of integrity should be relatively clear cut. If a question does leave you in a real dilemma (and some are designed to!) because your integrity leads you to an action that would be to the detriment of the company, there's nothing wrong with saying you'd take advice from a trusted colleague, manager or mentor.

What's important when giving an answer to questions like these is to show you're aware of the implications of your chosen action, and that you are weighing these up to come to a decision.

Coping ability

A popular question is to ask how you'd handle something happening at work that you didn't like. That could mean anything: new management, a team restructure, working style changes, revised responsibilities, different contract terms or cuts to promised training.

For example:

- ▶ 'A new manager starts. You find you really don't get along with them. What do you do?'
- ▶ 'How would you handle a difficult team mate who picks holes in your work?'
- ▶ 'How would you react if the commission structure changed halfway through the year and you were one of the few salespeople left with less money, instead of more?'
- ▶ 'If you felt disappointed at not getting the amount of training you were expecting during the year, how would you deal with it?'
- ▶ 'What would you say if I told you I wasn't going to offer you this job?'

WHEN HYPOTHETICAL BECOMES REAL

The last example is slightly different from the others. It's a scenario that could actually be put to the test in your interview, so be sure that your answer is something you can follow up on.

If you say 'I'd be disappointed, but I'd take it on the chin and keep looking for another opportunity this good,' – a provocative interviewer might say 'That's a relief; in that case I'm definitely not offering you the job.' If you then burst into tears, it's not ideal. If it was a bluff to put you under more pressure, you've shown you can't handle it.

The key with all pressure questions is to expect some and have prepared for some, so you don't react badly on the day to anything you're asked or told.

Insight

Your answers to most 'What if?' questions might depend on the detail. For the commission question, you might feel more strongly if this change would put your house at risk than if it means reining in your shopping habits. But the interviewer isn't that interested in getting into fine detail: they just want to know what sort of *strategies* you would use to deal with the situation.

Coping answers

How you handle negative situations in general is of much greater interest to an interviewer than how you would handle a particular detailed scenario.

So, when preparing for this type of question, try to think about your own coping style (or styles) in more general terms:

▶ Do you look into yourself for a solution, changing the way you behave or think?
▶ Do you attempt to use your interpersonal skills to influence those around you?
▶ Do you ask colleagues for their advice or support to solve a delicate problem?
▶ Do you look to the formal hierarchy, approaching your manager for advice?

Your answer could reveal a high degree of self-reliance and independence, or put you across as someone who can handle anything with the right support in place. The organization's ethos and the specific requirements of the job should, as always, influence how you answer.

Giving up something

...as in: 'Would you give up being in a band for this job?'

It's hard to know exactly what an interviewer wants to learn from your answer. Saying 'I'd do anything to get this job' might show eagerness, or that you can't stand your ground, or that you were insincere when you said being in a band meant a lot to you.

They may not be asking you to actually give it up, but just want to see what you say when put under pressure. It should not harm your chances if you state that your band activities don't impinge on your work performance.

'I've never been in a situation where I needed to. I've been with the band eight years now and you'll see from my track record that it's never affected my commitment to work or my job performance.'

You could also treat it as a serious question and ask for more information before answering. The interviewer may believe that you being in a band would conflict with work.

'That's an interesting question. Does my band membership give you any particular concerns about my work?'

Their answer: 'Well, the last person in this role was in a band, and played lots of gigs midweek. She was frequently not very effective at work the morning after.'

'Ah, I see. Well, I'd like to reassure you that in our band, all five of us work in demanding, full-time jobs. We rehearse on Tuesdays, but never perform midweek.'

Insight

Don't get too worked up about giving correct answers. While it would never be good to say you'd cover for a thieving colleague, more often there isn't one right answer to a 'What if?' question. How you reason and justify what you'd do in an unfamiliar situation is often just as interesting as the conclusion you reach. So, explain what you'd take into account, say how you'd weigh up your options, try not to be too black and white, and never just give one-sentence answers.

Even if the interviewer doesn't agree, or they'd teach you to do it differently in the job, it doesn't mean you've blown the interview.

16

Off-the-wall questions

In this chapter you will learn:
- *how to interpret and respond to unusual, seemingly tangential questions*
- *how they are usually used to test a candidate's ability to think on his or her feet.*

These are probably the hardest to prepare for, along with 'What if?' questions, in the traditional sense of preparing an answer that you could rehearse. And at least with 'What if?' questions you can take a guess at the likely topics. With off-the-wall questions you can never anticipate what you'll be asked.

How can you prepare?

For many people, it is enough simply to know that this type of question *might* be asked. By becoming more familiar with the format, you could certainly build a better framework for approaching whatever question you're faced with on the day, but you cannot possibly prepare for all of them. It shouldn't be an interview breaker if you don't give a model answer, but it's better if you don't sit there with your mouth open and eyes glazed.

WHY ARE THEY ASKED?

Awkward, surreal or seemingly impossible questions used to be a favourite for certain university entrance interviews, although they've become increasingly common in major corporations in recent years. How you answer can give great insight into how you think through a new or unusual problem. Often it's not so much the answer that counts but how you reached it.

If you're calculating or reasoning your way to the answer, don't sit in strained silence until you've got an answer to give. Work through it aloud, so the interviewer can understand how you're thinking.

Possible question types

The following are popular categories of off-the-wall questions:

▶ business
▶ personal
▶ estimation
▶ organization
▶ hypothetical
▶ logic problem
▶ summarizing
▶ comparative.

BUSINESS QUESTIONS

A consulting firm, for example, might like to hear how you would analyse and interpret information in order to make a recommendation.

The following is not a model question and answer, just an example of the kind of reasoning you might be expected to show for business-type questions.

Q: '*A sandwich business owner wants to create a chain and has three sites in mind for opening his second shop. He hires your consultancy to help him make this decision. This sheet shows his current store's location, size and performance. How would you advise him, and why?*'

A: You need to show you have taken into account all the information you've been given, that you understand the business implications and can create a logical recommendation from that. There isn't necessarily a right and a wrong answer: different people may well use different strategies, so it's important you give your reasoning.

'I'd recommend selecting the second site, because it's based on a high-footfall street in a business district so there would be thousands of potential clients around at lunchtime, the busiest time of day. Being the smallest of the three sites, it would also need less capital to set up and would have lower operating costs, and there is no direct competition in the area – all of which would generate maximum return on investment. You could also build a good mobile sandwich business from this convenient base, serving the offices in this area, which could help you get into a better position to open more stores in future.'

PERSONAL QUESTIONS

A company might like to see if you can think on your feet and whether you are easily fazed by an unexpected question about yourself. You could be asked almost anything so make sure your answer tells them something positive and relevant.

Q: *'If you had to create a nickname for yourself at work, what would it be and why?'*

A: Cheesy, but you could come up with a name based on your biggest achievement or your strengths: 'Digger. Because when things get tough, I always dig deep.'

Q: *'What's the single most interesting thing about you / that you've ever done?'*

A: Define interesting as something you'd never done before, or something unexpected. Perhaps you don't have a pilot licence, but could land a 747 because you have done a 747 simulator session; name the skills you used and what it taught you.

Q: *'If you could teach just one life lesson to your friends or family, what would it be?'*

A: Show your work philosophy: 'always do your best', 'work hard, play hard', 'nothing is for free', 'if it looks too good to be true it probably is'; anything that isn't immoral!

Q: *'If you won the lottery and didn't have to work, what would you do instead?'*

A: Come up with something challenging that uses your brain and skills, so you can talk about your brain and skills. Starting your own business suggests you may leave to do so one day; safer ground is unpaid voluntary work for a worthy cause.

Q: *'What was the most memorable thing about your journey here today?'*

A: Goes to show you don't just exist in a bubble, and take notice of what goes on around you. Safe to raise something you heard about on the news and that it was memorable because it interests you or is relevant to work.

With any personal question, the interviewer is looking less at your choice of answer and more at your ability to think on your feet or the reasoning behind it. Whatever the question, use it to bring in your key selling points, show your logic and reasoning, or give them an idea of your working style.

Q: *'On a scale of 1–10, how weird are you?'*

A: Yes, according to news reports, this *has* been used in real interviews. The question is: would you be a 2 or an 8? And how will your answer benefit you in this interview? It depends whose perspective you're taking, as weirdness is subjective.

Insight

With any question like this, always explain *why* you give yourself a particular rating. This takes the focus off the weirdness rating and gives you another chance to mention a positive trait. 'Great weird' or 'interesting normal' is definitely better than 'scary weird' or 'bore-you-to-sleep normal'.

Example

'In the eyes of my colleagues, probably about a 5 – they think I'm weird because I'm the only one who loves coming to work on a Monday!'

Or:

'I reckon about a 4 – I'm fairly mainstream in most respects, although colleagues tell me I have an unusual perspective on some things, particularly solving problems. They seem to think it's a good thing, as I often get asked for my opinion on other projects.'

Q: *'What would I find in your refrigerator right now?'*

A: If an answer cannot be verified, you don't need to volunteer the absolute truth if it won't enhance your image: 'Four bottles of white wine and a box of chocolates', or 'I don't know, my girlfriend/wife always gets my beer/makes dinner.'

The interviewer could be after almost anything: how healthily you eat, how good your memory is, whether you are indeed interested in cooking like you say on your CV.

It could also be used as a side door into questions they cannot legally ask, like 'Do you have children?' or 'What are your religious beliefs?', so a fairly vague answer is good. Mentioning 'insulin syringes', 'kosher chicken' or 'breast milk' would hand some things to them on a plate.

You could show good memory and organization by rattling off a list confidently. If your fridge contains something unusual, like maggots for a keen fisherman, then by all means mention this: it could be a good hook (forgive the pun) to help an interviewer remember you.

Example

'Not much by a Thursday; I shop at weekends for the whole week. Let me see... milk, yoghurt, butter, cheese and eggs. Some strawberries... carrots... broccoli. Half a cooked chicken and a cod fillet. Oh, and a compartment of black-and-white film. I'm a keen photographer and keeping it in the fridge helps preserve its quality.'

ESTIMATION QUESTIONS

These are questions for which there is most likely no fixed answer. The interviewer just wants to see how you approach calculating the answer.

Q: *'How many tennis balls could you fit into a Mini?'*

A: Reason aloud. Show the interviewer what factors you take into account, what assumptions you make, how you estimate or reason your way to the end figure. It's less important if your assumptions or calculations are correct (unless you claim to be a maths whiz), it's more about how you tackle it.

'Assuming it was a new Mini, a Cooper not a Clubman, for ease of calculation I'd estimate its length at 3 metres, width at 2 metres and height at 1.5 metres, giving a capacity of about 9 cubic metres. Assuming around two-thirds of that was taken up with the wheels, body, engine, driveline and seats, and that there were no people sitting in it, we'd have about 3 cubic metres of space for the balls.

'If we were using standard, unpackaged tennis balls that are not being compressed in any way, they'd be about 10 centimetres in diameter. We could fit around 1,000 per cubic metre if they were square – being round, they'd fit more snugly together so we could probably get an extra 10 per cent into the same space.

'So, 3 cubic metres would mean 3 times 1,100 balls, so I'd estimate 3,300 balls could fit in the car. Do you know if anyone's ever tried it and what the answer was?'

ORGANIZATION QUESTIONS

These may seem related to estimation questions, but these are less about your thinking processes and more about your organizational skills: how you would act as a project leader. You're not being asked to estimate an actual answer but to show an organized approach to allocating resources and finding out.

Q: *'How would you organize a team of ten people to find out how many cheese sandwiches were eaten for lunch in the Square Mile today?'*

A: You could do this in any number of ways, provided you use a logical approach and explain your reasoning.

'I'd start by brainstorming with the entire team to identify all the potential sources of information relating to cheese sandwich consumption. That way we'd be less likely to miss something. Let's say we came up with three main channels: pubs, cafés and restaurants selling cheese sandwiches; catering companies and canteens providing them for office workers, and finally people who bring their own cheese sandwich into work. I'd divide up my team of ten people so that three pairs start collecting the relevant information from each source, using the phone, Internet and personal visits as appropriate. I'd also have three people, one per channel, to collate the data coming back in. The tenth person I'd allocate as a trouble-shooter, to whom any and all issues and queries about data collection would be directed, so that we took a consistent approach to data collection, estimation and collation.'

HYPOTHETICAL QUESTIONS

These kinds of question may have a scientifically 'correct' answer but the interviewer's real interest lies in hearing the options you come up with.

Q: *'How might it be possible for someone to walk on water?'*

A: There is no single answer to this. But you might suggest:

▶ wearing big inflatable shoes
▶ freezing the water's surface
▶ walking over water inside a plastic sphere...

The answer could be any number of things: chances are, they're not looking for any particular one. Show your creativity and resourcefulness by approaching the question from different angles, and giving more than one option if you can.

LOGIC PROBLEM QUESTIONS

These are questions with a correct solution that you can use logic to figure out. You might be lucky and have heard the answer before, or it may come to you on the day, or you may not get the answer right at all. The key is to remain calm no matter what. An incorrect answer to a logic problem is normally unlikely to blow your interview, although for industries where a logical brain is desirable (software programming or consulting perhaps) then the stakes may be higher.

If you're interested in the solution to a logic question you can't answer, feel free to ask once you've completed your answer – the interviewer can only refuse. Some people advise against asking, but it can also show you're keen to understand and learn.

If you're daunted at the prospect of logic questions in your interview, you can find plenty of examples of lateral thinking and logic problems on the Internet.

Q: *'You work in a hospital pharmacy where someone has messed up the labelling on three boxes. One contains only blue pills, one holds only orange pills and the third has a mix of blue and orange pills – and no box has the right label on. You choose one box and can take out one pill without looking inside. Looking only at that pill, how do you place all the labels on the correct boxes?'*

A: 'Each box can only have one of two incorrect labels, so you should choose to open the box labelled Orange & Blue Mix. This label can only have been put on a box of single-colour pills, so as soon as you see one pill – say it's orange – you'll know the Orange Only label belongs on there. Of the two remaining boxes, one will have a Blue Only label – as it's wrongly labelled, it cannot possibly contain blue pills, so this must contain the mixed pills. The last box will therefore need the Blue Only label.'

Q: *'You are allowed to slice a round Christmas cake exactly three times, to divide it into eight equal pieces. How do you do it?'*

A: Cut it in half across the diameter, then half again, to make four equal pieces. The final slice should cut the cake in half *horizontally*, dividing it into two equal layers – giving you eight equal pieces.

SUMMARIZING QUESTIONS

These take a large amount of information, or a complex concept, and ask you to distil it down into something simple.

Q: *'I've just got back from a year in a remote village. Fill me in on what's happened in the UK / the world while I was away?'*

A: Decide which events to mention, there's only time for a few. It could be:

▶ those that stand out most in your mind and are completely unrelated

- events linked by a theme – political, human, business, climate, financial, etc.
- events relevant to this job, company or industry, if you can think of any.

If you are really well versed in current affairs, you might challenge yourself further by asking the interviewer which topics he would be most interested in hearing about. Whatever you choose, summarize what happened for each news item.

Example

'Well, it seems to have been a year of disasters, so I'll focus on those.

'In spring last year there was an oil rig explosion in the Gulf of Mexico, causing a massive oil leak which took months to cap – the environmental impact has been huge. Then last year's summer monsoon in Pakistan caused widespread flooding, with hundreds killed and a million losing their homes. In the autumn, an earthquake, tsunami and volcanic eruptions hit Indonesia, again killing hundreds and losing thousands their homes.

'Early this year, heavy rains caused the worst flooding seen on Australia's east coast for nearly a century, followed by an earthquake in New Zealand that nearly flattened Christchurch. And finally, a strong earthquake in Japan recently caused a tsunami that cost thousands of lives and homes, and left a nuclear reactor close to meltdown.

'Hopefully that's it for a while... and you've picked a good time to come back!'

COMPARATIVE QUESTIONS

These are when you're asked to compare yourself to something. That could be:

- an animal
- a vegetable
- a meal

- ▶ a fictional character
- ▶ a celebrity
- ▶ a tree
- ▶ another person
- ▶ a car
- ▶ almost anything, really.

You might think the interviewer has gone slightly mad, but in the interests of never wasting a question, come up with something. But don't just give the answer straight – give the person or thing the same positive skills and qualities you would like to portray.

If this kind of question scares you and you don't think you'll be able to think on the spot, take your priority key skills and think in advance of a few items, animals and people you can relate them to by way of preparation.

Example

'Hmm… (yes, do make it look as if you're giving it at least some thought) I think I'd probably be a bird of prey, because I'm not just good at viewing an overall situation from a distance but also at being able to focus in on smaller details when needed. Like a hawk diving on its prey, I really throw myself wholeheartedly into reaching my targets – but I'm still able to assess my progress and redirect my efforts if the target should move. So yes, I think I'd be a hawk – strategic, determined, tactical and adaptable.'

Insight

For a comparative question, choosing something unusual, rather than safe and predictable, can be a great hook to help the interviewer remember you afterwards. Be sensible though; if you compare yourself with an animal, choosing something with higher brain function like a bird or mammal is likely to be safer ground than an amoeba or jellyfish, unless you've got a very clever rationale up your sleeve.

17

Your own questions

In this chapter you will learn about:
- *what kinds of question you should and should not ask*
- *how to be alert to questions that arise during the interview itself.*

Time allowing, most interviewers will invite you to ask some
questions yourself. It helps if you've thought about this already,
rather than struggling to think of something sensible on the day.
There are many questions you could ask, but the ones you do
should…

- ▶ help you understand something important about the company so
  you can judge whether it's the right move for you
- ▶ demonstrate your genuine enthusiasm for the job and the
  company
- ▶ not show you up: make sure what you're asking isn't plainly
  answered on the home page of the company website, or in the
  brochure they sent you.

Insight
Always show, with any questions you ask, how interested you are in the
role and your long-term prospects with the organization, rather than in any
shorter-term gains.

How do they phrase their invitation?

- ▶ 'Do you have one or two burning questions I might be able to
  answer for you today?' means 'Make it quick, we're almost out
  of time; they'd better be important.'

- 'Do you have any questions for me about how this department or team operates?' means 'I'm offering you a chance for some specific detail but don't waste my time with more general questions.'
- 'Do you have any questions you'd like to ask?' means what it says, although try to limit it to a sensible number and keep an eye on the time.

Questions to ask

Choose no more than four or five questions that you'd really like answered, and keep them in priority order in case you end up short on time.

If these all get answered during the interview, and you worry it looks as if you haven't bothered thinking of anything to ask, you could say something like: 'Well, I was particularly interested in the detail of how the graduate training scheme works, but you've covered that for me already, thank you.'

PREPARED QUERIES

These could be about the organization, the role or the people. By making these sufficiently specific, it can subtly demonstrate your research and may even allow you to highlight additional skills. Your own questions can be reminders of the benefits you bring – for example: 'I am always keen to learn new and relevant skills. If I were to join the company, what opportunities…' Focus on longer-term questions that show you are serious about sticking around.

Insight
Some people believe that if you refer to yourself in the questions you ask, it will help the interviewer visualize you in the role. Whether that's true or not, you have little to lose by asking questions in this way.

SAFE EXAMPLES OF PREPARED QUESTIONS
- 'What kind of training and development opportunities will I have?'
- 'What sort of career paths have former holders of this job taken?'
- 'How fast can I expect to progress with your company?'

- ▶ 'I speak fluent French and Spanish. Would these skills be of use to the company at some point in the future?'
- ▶ 'Is it likely I'd be supported to gain relevant professional qualifications?'
- ▶ 'How, and how often, will my performance be reviewed?'

QUERIES ARISING DURING THE INTERVIEW

Be alert while the interviewer is talking and, if they mention something that triggers a query, note it down straight away so you don't forget later.

For example, you could ask about the interviewer's own background. This is particularly useful if you've find out that you have any points in common (companies worked for, industry experience, language ability, degree subject, interests, etc.) because you can ask if they found it useful in their role at the company. People naturally like those whom they perceive to be similar to them so it's a great chance to bring that home.

FEEDBACK QUERIES

These are a valuable addition to any interview, especially if all your other questions have already been answered. The structure of feedback questions should be prepared in advance, but the specifics may vary on the day.

Q: *'Do you have any reservations about my suitability for this role?'*

If this or a similar question results in one or more concerns being raised, don't feel crushed – it's a great chance to ask if you can address these concerns, or clarify any key points that haven't come across as well as they should.

Follow up with: *'May I briefly address your concern?'*

Q: *'What's the team culture like? From what you've seen, do you think I would fit in?'*

If the interviewer admits to having some concerns, ask if you can address them.

'We haven't touched on analytical skills [or any additional skill/ characteristic you have], yet it seems this would be important to this role. Is that so?'

If you get a positive answer, you can follow with: 'That's interesting because I developed strong analytical skills while in Mergers & Acquisitions, so I could support you with the process analysis project due next year.'

Q: *'I've only one more question and that is, what do you think? Do you think I'd be a good addition to the team?'*

This is important if you're going for a sales job – they'll want to see you can close a deal.

Insight

If you're after a sales role and try to close the deal during your interview, you could get a flat 'No'. Don't panic if you do: just ask politely which areas were causes for concern. If you can address these, by all means try; even if you can't, it's still worth asking because you'll definitely get better feedback in the interview itself than if you wait to ask until after you've got the rejection letter.

NEXT STEPS QUESTIONS

When all else fails, see what's coming next with a question like:

'You've already answered all the questions I had; nothing else springs to mind except to ask what happens next? When will I hear about the outcome?'

Questions to avoid

There are lots of questions you *can* ask at interview, but a number that you shouldn't – particularly at a first interview. Here are just a few examples:

- ▶ 'How much money/holiday/car allowance/free product/discount/ etc. do I get?'
- ▶ 'Hey, would you like to go for a coffee sometime?'
- ▶ 'What are your maternity benefits like?'
- ▶ 'Do you have a good counselling service?'

With the exception of enquiring about training and development opportunities, try to avoid questions like these, which focus more on what you want to get out of the company than on what you can offer.

FOCAL POINTS

- Prepare a handful of questions so you're not left scratching about.

- Focus on those that show your skills, research, or a long-term commitment to the company.

- Admit it if all your questions have been answered.

- Don't bring up selfish subjects like salary or benefits.

Part three
Action

18

....

Practicalities

In this chapter you will learn:
- *the importance of getting yourself organized before your interview, so that you are as calm as possible*
- *how to prepare a checklist/timetable for the period leading up to the interview.*

The practicalities of interviewing include knowing where you are going, getting there on time, arriving looking confident and with everything that you will need. Sort these in advance and you may be surprised how much more relaxed you feel, and how much easier it is to concentrate on what you'll be discussing when you arrive.

Reminders

Keep a reminder of the interview date and time in clear view (having checked it carefully to ensure it is correct), and set any diary reminders or calendar alarms as necessary to ensure you don't lose out by getting it wrong.

Driving

CAR MAINTENANCE

If you are driving, do simple things like checking tyre pressures and filling up with fuel the day before.

CAR CLEANING

It may sound like overkill, but if you're parking on company property make sure your car is clean – you never know who will see you get in and out.

> **Insight**
> On a practical note, cleaning your car the day before an interview makes it less likely that you'll dirty your interview clothes when getting in or out.

DRIVING DIRECTIONS

If you have none, print out directions from a site like streetmap. co.uk, the AA website, or Google maps well in advance. Running out of printer ink the night before an interview can be a nightmare.

Even if you print out (or are sent) directions, carry an up-to-date road map if you're driving. A diversion could get you lost. Sat nav may help, but isn't always reliable to the door of your destination, and technology can always go wrong.

JOURNEY TIMING

Check the directions make sense, then estimate how long it will take you to get there. Many travel sites will give you a time estimate but compare the local portion with your own experience and add a big safety margin to allow for delays on the day.

You should be aiming to arrive at least 30 minutes in advance so you have time to unwind from your drive and re-read your prepared statements and answers before reporting to reception.

TRIAL RUN

If you have time (and it's not too far away) a trial run may help you locate the offices or premises where you will be meeting and help you identify parking options if you can't park on site. Some industrial estates can be a warren of unmarked roads; finding the company you're looking for can take time.

If you can check the location out during working hours, you can also watch people coming in and out and see for yourself how smart or casual the dress code seems to be. You'll also probably get a general feel for the mood of the people who work there.

Public transport

JOURNEY TIMING

Check all journey times and connections well in advance, then check again the day before, just in case any timetables are affected by emergency works.

Allow for the almost inevitable delays, just like when you're driving. It's better to arrive at your final destination in time for a drink somewhere (think café, not bar) and to review your interview notes.

Insight

If you are tired when you set out on a long journey by public transport, and either intend to sleep or might do, play it safe and set the alarm on your mobile or watch. Missing your stop isn't a good start.

TIMETABLES

Keep timetables with you when you travel, with a back-up plan or an idea for alternative connections you could take if you miss yours or it's cancelled.

TICKETS

Book tickets in advance if you can, to avoid queues or delays on the day. If possible, try to reserve a seat in advance for a longer journey. Standing on a train for hours – or sitting in the carriage aisle – won't help you feel refreshed at the start of your interview.

Accommodation

If your interview is early in the morning and some distance away, think about staying overnight nearby. This reduces the chances of something going wrong on the journey there and means you should arrive feeling more refreshed.

This doesn't have to cost the earth – budget hotels are situated near many major routes and cities and prices are often lower if you book in advance or online. City centres can be a little more challenging price-wise, but you can often find a good deal on the outskirts and near good transport connections.

If you are attending interviews all over the country for company after company then it might not be feasible to stay away so much, but if there is a job you are particularly keen on then it's a worthwhile investment to help your interview get off to the best possible start.

Contact details

Ensure you have the name and ideally job title of the person you will be interviewed by, and check that the location of the interview is definitely where you think it is.

Keep a note on you of the interviewer's contact details, or at least the switchboard number of the premises you're visiting: if something goes wrong you need to be able to get in touch.

Clothes and possessions

If you're travelling straight from work to the interview, ensure you have your interview outfit with you or at least spare clothes if needed, such as a fresh shirt or spare tights, an umbrella, or anything else you may need to arrive looking well presented.

Take a mobile phone with you on the day if you can (though remember to put it on silent for your interview), and cash for sundries such as car parking, a phone call (in case of no mobile signal or battery), a last-minute taxi, a vending machine drink, or any other unforeseen reason.

Free your mind

This may sound like very basic commonsense preparation, and it is. However, when you are stressed or nervous, the simplest of things can get forgotten. Having a checklist and sorting out the practicalities in advance will help to increase your confidence and free up attention for what's really important.

Timetable

You may prefer to work with a timetable or checklist in the countdown towards your interview. Levels 1, 2 and 3 allow you to choose how much to focus on. Start with Level 1, then add elements from Levels 2 or 3. Below is a very basic example: feel free to adapt it or create your own to suit your circumstances. If any elements or techniques are unfamiliar, you can find more detail in later chapters.

Time before interview	Level 1	Level 2	Level 3
5–10 mins	– calm breathing	+ imitate confidence	+ positive reinforcement
15–20 mins	– enter reception – toilet break	+ read any company newsletters + notice company signs + small talk with other candidates, if a group interview	+ observe receptionist + note atmosphere + learn facts about other candidates, if a group interview
20–30 mins	– check appearance – ensure wearing interview shoes	+ study location and/or car park – does it appeal?	+ observe employees – are they happy?
30–60 mins	– re-read CV, notes and prepared answers – rehearse statements – no cigarettes, alcohol, smelly food		

travel time	– allow journey time + 50%		
before you set out from home	– shower, shave, teeth – outfit + shoes – spare tights/ shirt – comfy shoes, if needed – smart case or bag – cash – CVs/notes/ job ad – map/contact details – if driving, know where to park	+ read newspaper headlines/ listen to news + choose safe topic to discuss	
the night before	– limit smelly food – limit/abstain from alcohol – clean shoes – prepare outfit/ spare – rehearse answers, statements, check CV – print out CVs, notes, job ad, maps, etc. – find interview letter	+ read newspaper headlines/ listen to news + choose safe topic to discuss	+ check if any relevant news for industry

preparation	– know what to expect	+ further company and competitor research	+ interviewer research
	– company research	+ plan further answers	+ plan tough answers
	– prepare statements	+ refine any pre-work	+ key points to mention
	– plan basic answers		
	– note questions to ask		
	– clean outfit and spare		
	– practise confidence techniques, if needed		

FOCAL POINTS

- Having a checklist can help you to relax – you'll worry less about forgetting something.

- Arriving in good time makes it far easier to maintain a calm, confident demeanour.

19

What to wear

In this chapter you will learn:
- *that dressing conservatively/classically is usually best*
- *to be prepared for mishaps.*

Some people don't think twice about this – for others, it's the first question they ask. As first impressions are usually made before you've even had a chance to open your mouth, it's worth getting your clothing right.

You're right – your appearance should not make any difference to how well you can do the job. But it's a human, not a computer, who is making that assessment. They *will* form an opinion about the way you look, so don't overindulge your desire to stand out. At best you could get remembered for the wrong reasons; at worst you'll be judged through the veil of someone else's assumptions or prejudices. You might look boring, but it's better that your image says too little than too much.

The rule of thumb for interviews is to wear the smartest clothes you can that are appropriate to where you will be interviewed. Many interviews take place in an office of some kind, but you could end up anywhere: corporate HQ, a retail outlet, a manufacturing plant, a construction site, a workshop, an assessment centre or even in a hotel lobby.

Beware!

Some interview advice suggests calling in advance to ask about the dress code if you're not sure. While it might reassure you, there's also a risk this could backfire and make you look a little stupid. If you're competent to do the job on offer, surely you are competent to decide how to dress yourself in the morning? Think carefully before you call.

Individuality

Be careful of anything that screams 'individual'. Your ability is what you want to be remembered for after the interview, *not* your appearance.

If your normal style is ripped black clothing, pointed platform boots, spiked black hair, chains and multiple body piercings, all topped off with cosmetics that would make a mime artist jealous, be practical: will you blend into a typical interview environment? A navy suit and straight brown hair with no make-up might be a far safer bet, but if you really can't bear the thought of this, channel your creative energy into achieving a balance.

Insight

Not sure whether your style is appropriate? On the axis that runs from outlandish fashion at one extreme to ultra-conservative at the other, work out where you sit. Look around you at work, on the Tube, at the supermarket. Dressed in your choice of work or interview clothes, would you blend in or stand out? If you genuinely can't tell, ask a friend.

TONING DOWN

Your look can still be reflective of your personality without being a distraction. You're not looking to overturn your whole approach to fashion, just to dress appropriately on interview day. Try the following:

▶ Stick to black clothes, if that's what you like, but make sure they're smart.
▶ Lose the extreme footwear.
▶ If it's a natural colour for hair (just not *your* natural colour), you can leave it.
▶ Style hair more conservatively.
▶ Remove any piercings or chains that can be seen, apart from earrings. Use clear plastic retainers if you need to.
▶ Make do with a hint of dark eyeliner if you're into gothic make-up.
▶ Tattoos are best kept covered if possible.

Once you've got the job, plenty of time then to figure out how far to push your personal style in the workplace. Until then, play it safe if this job is what you really want.

Clothes

These should be smart and clean and ironed; and preferably be the smartest you have. That means daywear; leave evening dress in your wardrobe. If you really have nothing suitable, or haven't the time or money to buy anything specially, then think about borrowing – as long as it fits you properly.

TRENDS

There is much debate about exactly which clothes, cuts or colours to wear. Trends may change all the time, but your clothing should always take a supporting role. It should never be allowed to distract the interviewer from what you are saying. Plain, dark trousers or skirt, light shirt and dark jacket is a traditional and safe combination, although wearing the latest fashion shouldn't count against you unless it is very eccentric.

If you work in fashion or fashion retail, or are hoping to, the latest look will be desirable for interview. When applying to join a fairly conservative organization (look at the pictures of everyone on their website, what are they wearing?), classically styled clothes would be safer.

APPROPRIATE

While any fashion is fine, it needs to look tidy and not be inappropriately revealing. Revealing clothes are normally more of an issue for women than men (note to men: leaving your shirt unbuttoned to the stomach is not advisable).

Skirts that sit more than an inch or two above the knee are viewed by many as inappropriate for an office environment, while cleavage is always considered a distraction, whether the interviewer is male or female.

CASUAL

If you know (or guess from company photographs online) that the company has a casual dress policy, don't go to town. It is fine to turn up to interview wearing a suit even in offices where employees dress down, unless you have been instructed otherwise. There is nothing wrong with showing that you've made an effort and, after all, you are trying to make a good impression.

If you feel really uncomfortable with smart business wear, go for smart casual (jacket with trousers or skirt rather than a matched suit and a tie) – you can always take the jacket off if you want to blend in further. Wait until you've actually got the job before impressing them with designer ripped jeans and your favourite T-shirt.

Borrowed clothing is fine if you don't have a suitable interview outfit – but only if it fits you well, is comfortable to wear and isn't too old. A retro look may be fashionable, but if the cut and colour suggests your outfit has been around since the first time it was in fashion, leave it on the hanger.

Shoes

These should always be clean and polished (unless suede, although some people have been known to try). Unscuffed is better, but if you can't afford or borrow newer shoes, then try to colour in the scuffs as well as you can with polish or a pen.

Ladies, your interview heels might look fantastic but be impossible to walk in; if so, carry an alternative that you can walk in so that you don't turn up with blistered or uncomfortable feet. Limping can really undermine your attempts to look confident. Flip-flops or ballet shoes may be better comfort options than, say, trainers; don't forget you'll need to carry those trainers into the interview.

Insight
Think twice about packing smart shoes in your bag and wearing your scruffy, comfy options. When under pressure, it's quite easy to forget the smart shoes altogether. Play it safe: walk out of your home or workplace wearing your full interview outfit including shoes, then switch if you've got lots of walking to do.

Hair

Hair should be tidy, whatever the cut and colour, and it goes without saying that both it and the rest of you should be clean.

Plan to shave on interview day – or the night before if you can get away with it. Stubble (whether on faces or legs) can give the impression that you don't manage your time or don't care for your appearance.

Scent

You may love your favourite aftershave or perfume, the interviewer may not. Apply any scent well in advance and not in large quantities. If they can consciously smell you, that's not a good thing; if they have to open a window, that's a bad sign.

It goes without saying that scent should never be applied to cover up body odour – make sure you're freshly showered and use a good deodorant instead.

Bags

If you take a bag or case, make sure it's clean and smart. It should be able to hold whatever you need for your day, plus your interview notes and CV or application form.

If you do need to do a change of shoes, ensure you have enough room in the bag for whichever pair you're not wearing, without resorting to a plastic bag. Carrying plastic bags to your interview makes you look untidy and unprofessional, or as if you've done your shopping en route.

Underdressed or overdressed?

If on arrival you feel out of place because of your outfit, don't immediately start apologizing for how you look – unless you've failed to follow instructions you were sent about what to wear.

If you feel overdressed, remember that some people (and it's OK if you're not one of them!) wear jackets all the time, even for what they consider casual wear. If people can wear a suit to go clubbing or to go on a picnic, and still feel comfortable among a crowd of differently dressed people, why shouldn't you carry off the same at an interview?

Likewise, if you do feel a bit scruffy compared to everyone else there, then as long as you're neat and clean, there's no reason this should count against you. How you carry yourself can make a lot of difference to how your outfit may be perceived (or if it's even noticed at all).

Contingency plans

Any number of things could happen to your interview outfit, especially if you go to your interview straight from work. Even if you avoid tea, coffee or food on the day, other people can always oblige by spilling theirs over you.

Ideally, have a back-up outfit ready the night before in case you spill milk down your first choice or you get splattered by a passing car as you leave the house on a wet day.

While it's not practical to carry around a complete change of clothes with you, it is worth taking a spare clean top or shirt (and tie) in your bag. Ladies should think about carrying spare tights or stockings, if worn, and some clear nail varnish to stop ladders enlarging. Or just wear trousers or a long skirt to avoid the issue.

Insight

Many minor wardrobe malfunctions can be fixed on the spot with a small roll of Sellotape, so it's worth carrying. Hem coming down? Elastic gone? Flapping sole? Small tear? Tie pin lost? Shirt gaping? This temporary fix might crinkle a bit as you move, but it can help save your appearance for the interview. Just make sure you put it *under* whatever you're fixing so it can't be seen!

Carry an umbrella if there's even the slightest chance of rain. Even a pocket-sized foldaway will keep enough rain off you to stop you arriving with your hair plastered to your head and make-up running down your face.

Changes

If you know you are going to be doing some sort of on-site test, which may involve getting messy, bring an appropriate change of clothes (and shoes or wellies) and swap your smart clothes for these.

Read carefully any instructions for attending any assessment centre interviews and be clear about what to expect, so you can bring clothes for all the situations that may arise over the assessment day or weekend.

FOCAL POINTS

- Take careful note if you are given specific dress requirements.

- Always err on the smart, conservative side.

- Avoid wearing anything that could be a distraction for the interviewer.

- Have a pair of walking shoes if your interview pair aren't comfortable.

- If you look clean, neat and confident, you're unlikely to go far wrong.

- Always take an umbrella.

20

....

Getting into the
zone – confidence tricks

In this chapter you will learn about:
- *some techniques to help keep your nerves under control*
- *some longer-term ways of boosting your confidence.*

It is quite normal to feel nervous before an interview, even for experienced candidates. Low-level nerves can be good for focusing your attention and giving your abilities an edge but, when nerves tip over into panic, it can be crippling. Adrenaline gives your body enhanced performance, while your brain gets switched to automatic – and automatic isn't a great state for understanding questions or giving well-constructed answers.

The good news is that there are lots of things you can do to help reduce nerves. Probably the most effective way is taking the time to prepare fully for an interview, but there are also a number of tricks that may help.

Level 1

BREATHING

Take it from the yoga experts: it all starts with your breathing. This might sound almost too basic if you haven't tried it before, but focusing on your breathing can be very relaxing. As something we manage to do automatically even in our sleep, it takes a surprising amount of concentration to control your breathing – and while you're concentrating on that, it's harder to get wound up about impending interviews.

Draw in air in an exaggeratedly slow way, until your lungs feel as if they will burst, and then let it out very gently and steadily as if you're trying to blow a stream of tiny bubbles underwater.

A few repeats (or, if you have time, a few minutes of doing this) and you will notice your heart rate starting to reduce and, with it, that panicked feeling.

ABDOMEN

Similar to breathing control, another physical technique is to tense your abdominal muscles, hold them like that for ten seconds, and then relax. Repeating this several times can help remove the anxious sensation of butterflies in your stomach.

REHEARSAL

Perhaps it feels as if you've looked over your prepared answers a hundred times already, but this is something you can't overdo.

Insight

If you can, rehearse your statements and answers out loud. If there are specific words or phrases you are still tripping over, despite all the refinement and practice, change them for something that works better. Then rehearse that.

NOTES

Write some bullet points in large text on a couple of note cards or pieces of paper. This can be useful whether you are terrified your mind will go blank, or are just finding you keep forgetting one or two key points.

Stick to just two or three cards or sheets that you will keep on your lap to refer to: any more and it'll look like you're shuffling for a poker game as you desperately search for the one you want.

Having notes doesn't make you look less professional, provided you're not sitting head down talking to your lap or, worse, reading all your notes word for word. One quick glance down can help you remember an important point, example or series of facts.

Level 2

ACT

As if your life depended on it. Yes, act, as in action and actor. Like the way shaping your mouth into a smile can lift your spirits a little even when you don't really feel like smiling, learning to portray outward confidence will give your inner confidence a boost, too.

It is possible to simulate confidence and make it totally believable. An easy way to do this is to copy someone who appears confident: someone you know, someone who just walked past, a character in a film, whatever strikes you.

Think about how they walk, how they talk, how they move. Actions and speech are measured and unhurried. Head is held high, eyes level and there is no fidgeting. Copy it, pretend it, and if you practise it enough you should be able to 'fool' other people, especially if they don't know you well.

THINK

Your own nerves are often not as apparent to other people as you might think. It's rarely true that everyone can 'see your hands trembling' or 'hear your voice shaking' – most people simply don't pay that much attention. Convince yourself of that.

If your interviewer does pick up on your nerves, they may well make some allowance for it. Nerves alone don't mean you can't do the job you're applying for – just try not to let them get out of hand.

While pretending, don't let your new-found confidence tip over into arrogance.

Level 3

POSITIVE REINFORCEMENT

How to do it
This is about making a positive connection between your brain and your body, which you can summon up whenever you need it. The sooner you start practising, the sooner the connection will start to form – and the sooner you can start using it.

The 'body' part of the connection should be a small physical action that you choose: it can be anything, but should ideally be subtle and be an action that you don't regularly do. It might be flexing your fingers, making a circle with your finger and thumb, or pressing your heel into the floor.

The 'brain' part is thinking of a time when you felt really confident and really successful. It might be winning a go-kart race, holding your new-born child, getting your latest (and biggest) promotion or singing karaoke – you don't have to reveal to anyone what it is.

Picture this confident scene clearly and remember exactly how you felt at the time, throughout your body and mind. Then, holding this image and feeling in your mind, do the physical action. Repeat it again and again while focusing on how confident, strong and successful you felt.

How it works
The idea is that by repeating these two things together, a link will form in your brain and body. A sort of conditioning that, once established, means doing the physical part alone will stimulate the mental/emotional part.

You might choose to do this action the night before the interview, to help you feel more positive and therefore sleep better. You may do it mere moments before you walk into the employer's premises so you can keep on top of your nerves. If the movement is suitably subtle, you could even do it during the interview if your confidence flags.

You need to form the connection in advance; it's not something you can easily do at the last minute, and you need to keep the connection strong through repetition.

It's important to only do the physical action while recalling feelings of confidence and success. If you do the physical action while thinking of things unrelated to confidence or success, the link will lose its strength.

VISUALIZING SUCCESS

How to do it
Like the above, this technique may or may not capture your imagination, but it's worth trying in earnest to see if it does work for you.

Visualizing is about using your imagination to see and hear yourself having a successful interview; the assumption is that this 'practice' will make it more likely that you do well on the day, by boosting your confidence and positive attitude.

Make sure you have a few minutes of peace and quiet, and start by planting a basic image in your mind of what you'd look like, sitting there in the chair, if the interview were going well. It's important that this is a positive experience! Imagine how you'd appear confident, relaxed and smiling, perhaps leaning forward from time to time to show your interest. Add in colours, sounds, scents and emotions: how you would speak, how you would react calmly to challenging questions, how you would keep your feet still and your body calm – perhaps even how the chair feels underneath you.

Make every detail as realistic as possible, and let your daydream play out until you hear the interviewer offer you the job at the end. How do you feel at that point? That's the positive feeling you need to keep in mind throughout the visualization process.

How it works

It may take several minutes each time you do it, but if you're one of the people it works for, visualizing regularly can help you feel much more confident. The reasoning behind this is that by mentally rehearsing all aspects of your interview behaviour often enough, you literally start to feel as if you've done it all before. That means you can stay feeling and looking confident throughout, even though the actual interview is likely to pan out quite differently in reality.

The other way visualization can help nerves is because every time you think of interviewing, you associate it with a positive experience. Don't underestimate how useful that can be – particularly if you have suffered multiple rejections in the past.

Visualization isn't a technique you can adopt at the last minute, though; it takes repetition for it to build an effect, and even then it isn't for everyone.

FOCAL POINTS

- The interviewer often isn't as aware of your nerves as you are.

- Pretending to be confident has a very similar effect to actually being confident.

- Try different relaxation and confidence-building techniques: see what works for you.

- Some techniques need preparation: they can't be tried at the last minute.

21

···

How to appear/behave

In this chapter you will learn:
- **the basic rules of how to behave at interview**
- **how to master small talk**
- **how to build a rapport with your interviewer.**

There is so much advice and guidance floating around on paper and across the Internet about how to behave at interview that it's often too much to concentrate on at one time. Rather than overloading yourself with unrealistic expectations, particularly if you're new to the interview circuit, try building up your ideal interview behaviours in layers.

Level 1 explains the basics you should concentrate on first. Once you've mastered these you can practise adding Level 2 behaviours, and finally Level 3.

Level 1: The basics

LOOK INTERESTED

Perhaps this sounds too basic, but it means listen carefully. It's easy to be thinking so hard about what you're going to say that you forget to pay attention to what is being said.

Remain facing the person who is speaking, whether it's a solo interviewer, a member of a panel or another candidate during a group interview task. Keep your facial expression composed and, whatever you do, don't allow yourself to get distracted or yawn.

MAKE A REASONABLE AMOUNT OF EYE CONTACT

The interviewer may not know you and won't realize that you always look out of the window when you concentrate... they might just think you're bored or easily distracted. Perhaps you look down at your lap when nervous, but they could think you are lying.

Insight

If you don't feel comfortable looking people in the eye for any length of time, then practise – anywhere, with anyone. You don't need to challenge complete strangers to a staring match, just be aware and try to increase how long you hold people's gaze for.

A good trick is to focus on the bridge of the interviewer's nose; you'll appear to be looking them in the eye, but it will be a lot less distracting for you.

SMILE GENUINELY

This might sound silly, but when you're nervous or concentrating hard it's easy to forget to smile at all. However friendly or enthusiastic you feel inside, forget to match it with a smile and you'll risk coming across as emotionless, depressed or even angry – or possibly a charming combination of all three.

That smile needs to be genuine and there are two ways to achieve that. First, through practice, in front of the mirror, until you have a smile you can produce on demand that doesn't make you look as if you are ready for Halloween early this year.

Secondly, and probably preferable, is to make yourself *want* to smile. Inside your head, see the interview as an enjoyable experience and the interviewer as a friend. This can help you to speak more warmly and smile more freely. Note the 'inside' part – try to restrain yourself from kissing them hello on both cheeks, or going in for a mutual backslap at goodbye.

Insight

Don't imagine anyone naked.

Traditional advice suggests that picturing the interviewer naked will boost your confidence. Faced with a gorgeous-looking interviewer, your mind will definitely not be focused where it should. And for interviewers who are at best unattractive and at worst faintly repellent... well, derisive laughter is never appropriate. Nor is retching.

BE POLITE TO EVERYONE YOU MEET

From the cleaner to the managing director, from the PA to the hiring manager; everyone. Anyone you've come into contact with could be asked their opinion of you. Being polite includes:

▶ not arguing over spaces in the company car park
▶ treating security or reception staff with the same courtesy as the interviewer
▶ holding doors for everyone
▶ clearly greeting everyone with a smile and some eye contact.

DON'T FIDGET

This means watching out for your feet as well as your hands. You'll clasp your hands in your lap to keep them from shaking, but feet are often overlooked. Incessant toe tapping doesn't just betray your nerves; it can also be deeply irritating for the interviewer. Some people have also been found to move their feet more when they are lying, so still feet would be an asset.

Insight

Use the same tricks on your feet as you do on your hands. Try crossing your legs at the ankles to keep your feet together, or push your heels down hard onto the floor; anything to stop them from jigging about.

Level 2: Going a little further

MAKE CONFIDENT MOVEMENTS

This means slower, more measured gestures or adjustments in position. The same goes for how you walk. This helps your body language get 'in sync' with what you're saying and that makes it more likely your answers will be considered trustworthy.

EASY SMALL TALK

It's likely you're one of three types and see small talk as either a) impossible, b) pointless or c) simple.

Whether you enjoy it or not, your interviewer is quite likely to use small talk as an interview tool – either as an artful way to establish a bit more about your personality, communication style, interests or opinions, or as a way of easing you into the main part of the interview without being abrupt. So you will need to be at least passably good at it while keeping your eye on ways to sell yourself if the chance arises.

Incidental small talk

There are two types of small talk. This type tends to focus on the here and now: How was your journey? Isn't it great not to have snow on the ground any more? Where have you come from today? Were you listening to Radio 1 on the way in?

Focused small talk

The other type of small talk may be natural, or it may be a little more contrived and involve topics that bear no relation to the job in hand. Perhaps the interviewer wants to know whether you take an interest in all aspects of the real world around you. So this could be more like: 'Did you see that TV documentary last week about the river of blood?' 'What caught your interest in the papers this week?'

Practice

A great way to improve at any kind of small talk is to do it regularly. That might mean forcing yourself to do something that doesn't come naturally: engaging people in casual conversation at every opportunity. That means everyone you meet during the day, from shop assistants to people in queues, from taxi drivers to strangers standing next to you in the pub. The more you do it, the easier it will get.

Headlines

The key to tackling the 'Are you interested in the world around you?' type of small talk is to have a rough idea of what to say if asked – to have an opinion. Make sure you've read a current paper, listened to or watched the news.

Familiarize yourself with the main headlines and pick out one or two that particularly interest you and which you could talk a little about. If current affairs (e.g. legislation) might affect the company you are applying to, make sure you look into it a little deeper if you have time. If current events influence one of your main interests or hobbies, make sure you can explain briefly what the issue is and why.

LISTEN ACTIVELY

We've already talked about looking interested and listening carefully. Active listening involves not just sitting with your mouth shut and ears open, but demonstrating through subtle signals that you hear and understand what is being said.

These actions are often unconscious and can include tilting your head to one side to show you are listening, gentle nodding to show understanding or agreement, small changes in facial expression to reveal emotions such as sympathy or surprise, shifting position or leaning forwards slightly to indicate you are interested, and so on.

Active listening is almost like giving the speaker encouragement to go on – but do make sure it really is subtle. Too many concurring noises like 'mmm' and 'yes' can make you sound bored or insincere. If you grin like an idiot and nod vigorously at everything, rocking backwards and forwards in your seat, the first reference an employer may want from you is a medical one.

APPROPRIATE GESTURES

▶ Sitting as still as a statue throughout any conversation can make you appear uncharismatic if not totally lacking in personality.
▶ Emphatic gestures allow you to underline enthusiasm, excitement, frustration, and other states without having to spell them out.
▶ Do allow your body to move about a bit and help express words non-verbally, but keep your gestures in check. You don't need to look like a fitness video to make your points.

RELAXED BUT ALERT POSTURE

This means sitting upright, but not with your shoulders tense and back rigid as if you have drawing pins sticking into it. Hold yourself straight, but with your shoulders lowered so you look at ease. Focus on holding this position calmly, with no fidgeting.

Level 3: Finishing touches

OBSERVING THE INTERVIEWER

So far, you've been focusing purely on your own behaviour and appearance. How can you be 100-per-cent sure that you're getting it right when you do? As you move up a level, your behaviour should include checking for feedback from the interviewer.

Positive feedback

If the interviewer is providing positive feedback – nodding, smiling encouragingly, gesturing for you to continue, looking interested – then the most likely interpretation is that you are making a positive impression.

Negative feedback

When the interviewer gives feedback signs of the type you've been trying to avoid giving yourself – fidgeting, looking around, yawning or checking their watch – then it's time to change what you're doing. Chances are you're taking too long to get to the point, so modify your approach to be more concise.

Frowning and head shaking would suggest the interviewer doesn't agree with what you are saying. Be careful: this doesn't mean you are wrong and should instantly change your mind. You can resolve this another way, perhaps by pausing and saying something like 'You don't seem to feel the same way?' – which gives you a chance to set them straight if they have misunderstood, or to understand their perspective if they have a different viewpoint.

BUILDING A RAPPORT WITH THE INTERVIEWER

By implementing Levels 1 and 2, you should already be building a level of rapport with the interviewer through techniques such as active listening and eye contact.

Now, instead of only demonstrating how brilliant you are, it's time to show the interviewer how very much alike you both are. People naturally feel more drawn to those they feel they have a lot in common with.

Mirroring

A great technique for building rapport is called 'mirroring', which is when you subtly imitate the interviewer's behaviour. If they start to speak a little faster and more excitedly, you can let some of this creep into your own voice, too. If they lean forward, you can lean in as well. If they cross their legs with one foot pointing towards you, you make the same move, just as if they were looking in a mirror. Masters of rapport-building techniques claim that you can even synchronize breathing to great effect, but how far you take it is up to you.

Insight

Mirroring, to be effective, must not be overt. If the interviewer realizes what you are doing, it loses impact. If they have a warped sense of humour, they might start producing increasingly awkward moves just to see to what lengths you will go to copy them.

Be adaptable

Behaviour rarely remains constant for long periods of time, so make sure you stay alert to all changes in the interviewer's demeanour. It's all very well to reflect their enthusiasm as it builds, but remember to check how it's holding up later on. If they're no longer showing enthusiasm, your behaviour could end up as the opposite of your interviewer, which can start to reverse the rapport-building process.

If your interviewer wants to test you in a pressurized situation, they may deliberately reject your rapport-building attempts. An easy way for them to do this is simply not to respond to your mirroring, or they may try to break out of the rapport by always doing the opposite of your behaviours.

Flexibility is also important when it comes to group situations such as panel interviews, social events, group interviews and group exercises at assessment centres. Being aware of others, sensitive to their feedback signals and able to adjust your own behaviour accordingly is a very valuable skill. This can take time to master though, especially when you're also trying to think of the best response to a question or group task challenge.

FOCAL POINTS

- Don't overload yourself: master the basics before moving up a level.

- Non-verbal communication can enhance or undermine your verbal answers.

- Building rapport can help you influence and even control the interviewer.

- Anything you struggle with, start practising in your everyday life.

- All behaviours must be subtle if they are to be effective.

22

How to sound

In this chapter you will learn:
* *that* how *you say something is as important as* what *you say.*

We've already focused on how to behave – now it's time to look specifically at speaking.

There are two general rules: say it *slowly* and say it *clearly*.

Speaking is easy to practise at home. Stand in front of a mirror or video camera (or a friend, if you are brave and they are willing), while rehearsing your key statements and answers. Listen to yourself carefully, either live or in playback mode, and think about how you are coming across.

It can feel odd, listening to yourself, but don't try to give yourself a general mark out of ten. That can knock your confidence and will tell you very little about which aspects you could improve. You'll need to keep an eye on the following six factors: tone, speed, variation, pauses, simplicity and length.

Insight

If you've never focused on your speech before, there can be a lot to think about all at once. So you don't get overwhelmed: pick one or two of the easier aspects and start with those. Once you feel as if you've mastered those, try moving on to the next thing.

Level 1

▶ Keep your throat relaxed and speak in a low tone. This is much easier on the ear of the listener and makes you sound more confident.

- ▶ Use simple words and phrases. You are less likely to stumble over them on the day – you will spot troublesome words or phrases during rehearsals and weed them out.
- ▶ Pause occasionally. It's easy to talk faster and faster, so you end up sounding out of breath or impossible to understand.
- ▶ Keep every answer as short as possible while still covering the most relevant points.

Level 2

- ▶ Don't go monotone. While keeping your tone low and speech slow, allow yourself to talk faster and in a slightly higher pitch at times, to show your enthusiasm.
- ▶ Respect the interviewer's pauses. If they stay silent once you've finished your answer, don't break it. If it's not a question, stay quiet.

Level 3

- ▶ Subtly reflect the wording, pace and tone of the interviewer as a way of bringing them into rapport with you.
- ▶ Use controlled variations in tone and controlled pauses to emphasize your points and to keep your answers sounding lively and interesting.
- ▶ It's a balancing act: you should rehearse until you sound confident and feel as if the words are coming easily to you, but then stop before you end up too word-perfect.
- ▶ If you worry that you are starting to sound too slick, like you're reciting mini speeches, you can always throw in a couple of extra pauses while you speak. Pauses will help you look as if you're considering what to say, while also slowing you down. Practise your pauses, too, so they are effective in the way you want them to be.

FOCAL POINTS

- How you speak is as important as what you say.

- Be aware of how you speak: use the mirror or a video to assess your skills.

- Performance only improves with practice: reading is not enough.

- Identify just one or two improvements at a time, so you're not overloaded.

23

Stick to the plan

In this chapter you will learn about:
- *keeping to your plan*
- *leaving gracefully.*

Having done all this preparation, use it: don't let it sail out of your mind as you sit down in the interview chair.

If you panic on hearing an unfamiliar question, and start winging it, you'll soon lose your way. Listen carefully to each question, think it through against the answers you have already prepared, and construct the most suitable answer you can. Many of your interview questions will sound different to the ones you've prepared answers to – but will likely be seeking to uncover similar information.

> **Insight**
>
> If you worry that you may go to pieces on the day, then lots of practical rehearsals (or even a role-play interview with a trusted friend) are a great way to drum the right behaviour into your head. Practising turns behaviour into habit, instead of being something that has to be consciously remembered.

Memory tips

Make brief notes of key points, and refer to them during the interview if needed. This is perfectly acceptable: it's a sign of preparedness, not weakness. Sometimes you won't even look at the notes once – just having them on your lap will be enough to avoid a mental block.

Ensure you always provide proof to go with each claim you make, using the examples you've prepared. Keep notes on your lap as a prompt and make sure you have at least two or three for every skill. Talk about the most recent first, and only use older ones if asked to supply more proof. Try to avoid anything over two years old, unless it was specific to a particular role you did some time ago.

Try to include one positive point about what you'd bring to the company in every answer, even if you are asked about weaknesses or past failures. End with how you have improved your skills, what you have learned or how you work differently now, and how that has benefited your current employer. Answers should never be left hanging on a negative.

You may get some warning when the interview is coming to a close: things like 'I have one last question for you' are a bit of a giveaway. In this case, answer the question briefly and add a summary of the benefits you would bring to the company. It's a neat way to wrap things up and remind them of all the good things you've mentioned during the interview.

A smooth finish

With the relief of the interview itself ending, remember what you've learned. Be positive about the experience, with whomever shows you back to reception or out of the door. Don't relax or let your guard down, or admit it was terrifying: *it isn't over yet.* Don't let your relief translate into waffle that reveals something you didn't intend to: 'Thank God that's over; I was terrified. More than I thought possible. S'funny, it's only an interview but I was shaking all over. Worse than the day I got banged up.' Oops.

Insight
▶ If you feel it went well, smiling is permitted.
▶ If you feel it didn't go well, smiling is essential.

If you can't trust yourself, have the right comments ready and waiting in your mind. If the person asks how you think it went, give an answer that focuses on the positive and on how much you want the job. Something like 'It was really interesting. I've been wanting to get more of a feel for the company and this has really helped,' doesn't give anything away.

If you're feeling bold enough, and have the opportunity, try asking the person who shows you out how long they've been with the company and what they feel it's like to work in. Most people love to talk about themselves. Provided you listen actively, it may not only get you some more useful information about the company, it could also help you escape any further questions and avoid putting your foot in it.

Leave gracefully

That means no muttering, cursing, punching the air/wall/receptionist (delete as appropriate), holding your head in your hands, skipping, crying, pulling your shirt over your head and running around the car park (even if you feel like it), and no fat cigars. Definitely no calling a friend and saying loudly what a crap interview you just had, what a loser/bitch/geek/dimwit the interviewer was.

Even once you're in the street outside, you never know who works for the company and who might overhear you. Get clear before you let your guard down.

Personality

Once you're confident you can stick to the content of your answers, and deliver them in an effective way, and maintain your guard throughout the process, you can start to experiment with how much personality you inject into proceedings.

For example, don't aim to present yourself as a comedian, but if you strike up a good rapport with the interviewer there's no reason why you can't inject a little warmth into your answers with gentle and appropriate humour.

Humour is easiest to use when being interviewed by one person, because you can easily see their response to your warm-up efforts. Far harder is using humour with a panel of interviewers, because you're unlikely to establish a close rapport with everyone and their senses of humour are bound to differ.

Humour (especially dry) is probably best avoided for telephone interviewing, as you can't see the normal visual clues that someone is being light-hearted rather than serious.

FOCAL POINTS

- Don't let things slip on the day: keep in mind all your preparation.

- If necessary, keep some preparation on notes that you can take in with you.

- Keep practising your interview skills until conscious behaviour becomes habit.

- Whatever has happened, smile and finish gracefully.

- Never let your guard down too soon.

- Once you're using all you've learned, try injecting more of your personality.

24

Troubleshooting

In this chapter you will learn what you can do if you:
- *are going be late or can't attend your interview*
- *face a hostile or difficult interviewer*
- *feel you've made a poor impression in one area*
- *have an unsuccessful interview.*

Interview day is a Murphy's Law favourite – even if it doesn't happen often, something is likely to go wrong one day. It may help you stay more calm and professional if you've at least considered the possiblity of a problem arising.

Problems getting there

If you're the kind of person to whom the unexpected does seems to happen a lot, your planning and timing may need looking at again. Otherwise, take it in your stride. Perhaps:

- ▶ you start to run late, despite all the buffer time you planned in
- ▶ a fellow commuter spills coffee all over your lap on the train
- ▶ you're involved in some kind of accident
- ▶ your child is ill and you cannot leave them with anyone.

First, you need to work out whether you are going to arrive late, either because of the incident itself (cancelled train) or as a result of sorting it out (buying new trousers).

RUNNING LATE

If you think you will be late, but can still make it, then as soon as possible:

- ▶ call and ask to speak to the interviewer or a colleague
- ▶ mention when your interview is, apologize once, say you have been delayed (don't go into detail) and give your estimated arrival time
- ▶ ask if they could see you at or after that time instead
- ▶ if that's not possible, ask if you could postpone
- ▶ try not to hang up without a confirmed alternative time or date.

If you have to rebook, aim for the earliest possible date.

UNABLE TO MAKE IT

If you can't make it at all, call the interviewer as soon as possible:

- ▶ Say that you can no longer make the interview day and apologize sincerely.
- ▶ You don't have to explain in great detail why. These things happen sometimes. Stay professional.
- ▶ Say you are still very interested and ask if you can reschedule.
- ▶ Try not to put the phone down without agreeing a new time.

EXPLAINING WHY

If children or other personal reasons are the cause of your lateness or inability to attend an interview, then consider carefully whether you want to advertise this fact, even if the circumstances are truly exceptional.

Whether you have children or other dependants is not something you should be asked during an interview, nor are you legally obliged to answer if asked. However, if you can't make the interview and cite dependants as the reason, you could call into question your ability to manage work around your personal life.

Insight

More acceptable reasons for lateness might include car problems, or, for non-attendance, that your current employer urgently needs your presence at work today for a particular meeting/activity. Be wary of fictional public transport problems: these can be checked.

Remember your story! Don't catch yourself out with your own lie.

Scary interviewers

Scary interviewers fall into more than one category. Some come across as scary without intending to, while others deliberately cultivate an intimidating style of questioning and behaviour to see how you'll react.

OPENLY HOSTILE INTERVIEWERS

This is often a deliberate tactic to put you under stress – either that or the interviewer is having a very bad day and is letting it show.

Dealing with it
- ▶ Don't be hostile or defensive in return, it won't help.
- ▶ Do not treat it jokingly, even if it is just a technique: the interviewer still expects serious responses.
- ▶ Look past the hostility: focus on answering the questions.

If it seems like the interviewer really is hostile towards you, don't be distressed if the interview doesn't go so well... It's great practice, and would you really want to work for them?

INDIFFERENT/DISTRACTED INTERVIEWER

This is when you get no feedback clues, or they seem to be concentrating on something else. This could be a deliberate tactic to see how you cope, but it may be that they are under pressure or just come across that way.

Dealing with it
- ▶ Maintain your own focus and demeanour.
- ▶ Continue to answer questions just in case they are listening!

If the distractions become really great, you could pause *once* to ask politely if there's something that needs their urgent attention. Sometimes this is enough to bring someone's focus back.

SILENT INTERVIEWER

This could be the interviewer who gestures you in, shakes hands, indicates for you to sit, and then, apart from wording their questions, says absolutely nothing else. No feedback. This tends to make people feel very uncomfortable.

Silence is a very effective tactic, because the common reaction is to try to fill the gap. The temptation is to say too much, to give extra unnecessary details, to confess things you shouldn't. All because you can't bear the silent treatment.

Dealing with it
- ▶ Fight the urge to blab: stop talking when you'd planned to.
- ▶ If the interviewer stays silent, just give a calm, friendly smile that shows 'I'm all done, thanks' and wait for the next question.

••
Insight
You can still build rapport with a scary interviewer, if you are experienced. Try subtly mirroring the gentler aspects of their behaviour, and overlay this with more positive behaviour, aiming to bring them into sync with you rather than the other way around. At least you are setting them a good example.
••

Clawing back the positives

If something doesn't go so well, or you feel you didn't answer a question very well, you can simply bring it up – directly or indirectly.

DIRECT APPROACH

Ask the interviewer outright if they agree that your answer/comment/statement wasn't so good, and ask if you can briefly address it. If they refuse, so be it.

INDIRECT APPROACH

If you can't face directly raising a negative or are not sure if the interviewer will agree with your assessment, wait until it's your turn to question the interviewer and ask if there was any area of your interview or any aspect of your skills and experience that they are concerned about. Then ask to address those areas.

THE RISKS

Either approach can be risky:

- ▶ You are drawing attention to something that isn't positive. However, being aware of your performance is a positive trait.

- ▶ The interviewer may – after you've highlighted your weakness – refuse to let you address the point again. At least you tried!
- ▶ The interviewer may raise something you weren't expecting to hear. If this happens, address the issue like you would for any other feedback.

Extending the interview

You can also extend the interview artificially by writing a short thank you note. While thanking them for their time, you also:

- ▶ mention you are still very interested in the role and company
- ▶ restate your strongest points
- ▶ provide any extra relevant details or answers you promised.

Insight

- ▶ Feel comfortable sending a thank you note, if you think it's appropriate. It could be a useful way of keeping your name at the front of their minds. It would be rare that you *aren't* offered a job simply because you sent a polite thank you note.

Learn from yourself and others

Unsuccessful interviews can be very disheartening, but if you learn from the experience it may help you when you find your dream job opportunity. Real interviews are usually the best way for you to practise and improve.

LEARN FROM YOURSELF

Get in the habit of making a few short notes as soon as you're out of the interview situation. It needs to be really fresh in your mind.

Useful details to consider include:

- ▶ what went well
- ▶ what went not so well and how you might have done better
- ▶ areas where you're really not sure how you performed
- ▶ questions you hadn't prepared for: add them to your list
- ▶ job-specific queries you couldn't answer but should have
- ▶ what you'd do differently if you faced this interview again.

Other things it can help to note down include:

- ▶ anything you saw at the company that made you want to work for them less or more
- ▶ anything you'd want the company to explain or address.

Learning from yourself is the only way to increase your self-awareness and understanding.

LEARNING FROM OTHERS

The interviewer

Don't be afraid to ask for feedback at an appropriate moment. If you think everything went OK but you didn't make it through to the next stage of interviews, you can try calling or emailing (politely) to ask what else you could do to improve your future chances, because you are still keen on working for the company.

Be prepared to deal with the feedback you get; no matter what you hear you should not allow yourself to become defensive. If someone takes the time to speak with you, make sure you note down all their comments – word for word if possible – so you're absolutely clear later on what you have to do.

The recruitment consultant

A recruitment consultant may be prepared to be much more frank and detailed with you. They may also be able to suggest ways to improve next time.

Recruitment consultants are well rewarded for successful placements, so they will usually have a vested interest in seeing you do well. Some may even offer interview practice for less experienced candidates.

ACT ON WHAT YOU LEARN

After going to the effort of seeking feedback, make changes.

Short term

Book a place on a course, organize some sort of practice (e.g. role play with a friend) or do some focused work with a coach or mentor. Practice can also include more interviews, or meeting up with more agencies to get a feel for what's out there and how you might compare with other candidates.

Longer term

There might be a work-based skill or type of experience that you lack, which it would really benefit you to gain before trying to apply for similar roles.

If there are gaps in your skill set that need plugging, be realistic about whether you meet the next job spec sufficiently well for your application to stand a good chance. Spend your precious time gaining the skills or experience you need to stand a good chance of getting the job you want.

KEEP YOUR CV UPDATED

Don't forget your CV in all the excitement of your interview. Use interview feedback to update your CV as well, so that everything stays consistent. If there is lots of interest from interviewers in a specific area of your expertise, elaborate on it a bit more in your next CV. If you get a particularly good response to one of the skill examples you give during an interview, make it more prominent in your next CV.

FOCAL POINTS

- If you think you'll be late, phone as soon as you can and keep your explanation brief.

- Try to agree a new interview time BEFORE you hang up.

- Remember your 'story' if you give a false reason for a delay.

- However awkward the interviewer, focus and answer calmly.

- Never assume a scary or hostile interviewer is merely joking.

- Don't reflect a difficult interviewer's style; you may seem combative or not interested in the job.

- Prepare positive spin to cover your weak points.

- Addressing a potential issue at the end could help you make a more positive impression before you go.

- Assess your own performance as soon after the interview as possible.

- Ask the interviewer for feedback and respond to criticism positively.

25

Conclusion

Job hunting, or progressing your career – whatever you prefer to call it – is an ongoing process. Your CV is the starting point for, and your final interview the culmination of, every cycle you go through.

The preparation required to get an edge over everyone else during the interview stage can take up a fair amount of time to start with, but it's worth doing properly. A job can make the difference between living and existing; a full-time job may mean spending most of your waking hours at work. Whatever your motivation to apply for a role, it makes sense to give yourself the best chance of getting the one you really need or want.

Following a practical approach to interviewing, like the one described in this book, means you will get better every time you do it. The more practice you gain writing CVs and handling interviews, the faster you'll be able to prepare for your next one. Every job you land, each new skill you learn, every piece of knowledge you acquire along the way, the greater your employability and so the easier your next move.

The interview skills you start learning today will help to shape every job or career move you make in future. You just need to decide what that next move should be.

For up-to-date information and, resources about CV writing, interviews and career development, please visit www.teachyourself.co.uk and click on the Business channel.

Index

Credits

Front cover: © iQoncept - Fotolia

Back cover: © Jakub Semeniuk/iStockphoto.com, © Royalty-Free/ Corbis, © agencyby/iStockphoto.com, © Andy Cook/iStockphoto. com, © Christopher Ewing/iStockphoto.com, © zebicho – Fotolia. com, © Geoffrey Holman/iStockphoto.com, © Photodisc/Getty Images, © James C. Pruitt/iStockphoto.com, © Mohamed Saber – Fotolia.com